JUDAH P. BENJAMIN
Statesman of the Lost Cause

BY
ROLLIN OSTERWEIS

Foreword by
HORACE D. TAFT

Illustrated

G. P. PUTNAM'S SONS
NEW YORK :: LONDON
1933

COPYRIGHT, 1933, BY ROLLIN OSTERWEIS

All rights reserved. This book, or parts thereof, must not be reproduced in any form without permission.

PRINTED IN THE UNITED STATES OF AMERICA

For DAYTON

FOREWORD

How time changes all things and especially our opinions of men and measures. When I think what we were taught in the time of fierce passions after the Civil War, taught about the personal motives of Jefferson Davis and his associates, about the treachery of Andrew Johnson and the necessity and the justice of the reconstruction measures, and then think of the revision or reversal of these opinions which time has brought, it brings home the modesty which ought to characterize our present judgments and especially our judgments of men and their motives.

It is a great thing that the passions of the Civil War have cooled and that we can study with charity and without bias the point of view and the springs of action of the great men of the time, both North and South.

Of course, for us of the North the Southerners who first received due recognition were the warriors. For one thing they did brilliant fighting which all could understand. For another thing we think of the soldier as obeying orders and we relieve him in our minds of responsibility for the policies which we condemn. Thus our bitterness was reserved for the civilians, and boys of my time were taught to regard as a peculiarly wicked traitor that very conscientious and high-minded gentleman who, with many mistakes and with fatal faults of temper and temperament, yet guided the Confederacy with single-minded devotion to duty as he saw it. The persecution of Davis by the North made him a martyr, and the memory of the man who through the second half of the Civil War was quite unpopular with the Southern people has become a symbol of the lost cause. The whirligig of time brings in its revenges.

No such good fortune came to Judah P. Benjamin. He gave without stint of his enormous vitality and brilliant ability. Although his advice was sought on all subjects by his chief, to whom he was absolutely loyal, diplomacy was his chief sphere of action. In this sphere fate had stacked the cards against the Confederacy. The North held the good hands and while Charles Francis Adams had the playing of those hands there was no hope of success for the South. Her military success was never quite sufficient to move John Bull from his platform of neutrality and the question of negro slavery, especially after the emancipation proclamation, was an insuperable handicap to every Southern diplomatist. Yet it is hard to see how any man could have done better than Benjamin. He was one of the few who foresaw the length and the desperate chances of the war. His plan for exporting a vast quantity of cotton to England as a reserve on which to draw for the expenses of the war seems at this date to have been the highest wisdom. He was one of the first to recognize the need of using the negroes as soldiers. Mr. Osterweis tells the circumstances under which he resigned as Secretary of War, circumstances which indicated a higher degree of patriotism than any feats of brilliancy on the battle field.

But the chief adviser of an unsuccessful administration inevitably was unpopular. He and Seward were very different in character and mind. Yet in certain things they were alike. Each was a trusted adviser of his chief. Each was loyal to that chief in success or failure. Each was the object of bitter attack on the part of those who opposed the administration, but who could not reach the head of it, and each was supported and sustained by his chief to the end with the unswerving trust he had deserved. That Benjamin's unpopularity was the result of his official position and not of his personal qualities his whole life shows.

When we come to his personal career we can find no parallel. It is brilliant and fascinating. An alien by birth and race in the exclusive and aristocratic society of Louisiana, he rises to the very top of the bar, first in Louisiana and then in the nation, and to the leadership of state politics, and to the forefront of orators and statesmen of the South in the United States Senate. Then follow the four years of statesmanship and diplomacy. Finally a fugitive from his own country, he begins at the age of fifty-five a new career in a foreign land and, beginning at the bottom of the bar, in an amazingly short time rises to the very top. It is safe to say that no English lawyer was more respected and beloved at the time of his retirement. The manifestations of this respect and love amaze us still when we think that only sixteen years elapsed between the time he landed on English shores and the time when the English bar as one man united to say an affectionate farewell. Surely a unique career and one proving an amazing combination of qualities of mind and heart and character.

Mr. Osterweis has done a great service in telling briefly and vividly the story of his life.

HORACE D. TAFT.

THE TAFT SCHOOL,
WATERTOWN, CONN.
July, 8, 1933.

PREFACE
☆

THE purpose in writing this book was to present a concise, readable account of a highly colorful career. There is probably no more fascinating figure in our history than the greatly neglected Premier of the Lost Cause. Indeed, the story of his life reads like an excerpt from the Arabian Nights, shifting from one stirring scene to another.

Benjamin was born in the West Indies, of British parentage and under the British flag. He obtained his early education in the Carolinas and passed his college days at Yale. Coming to New Orleans in the poorest circumstances, he rose to be the leader of the Louisiana Bar. In his spare time he developed a great sugar plantation and became a father of the cane industry in his state. Entering politics, he graduated from the State Legislature to the Senate at Washington. For ten years he championed the cause of the South, his brilliant oratory ringing time and again thru the Halls of Congress. During those years he headed the first group that attempted to build an isthmian canal in Central America. Besides, he devoted sufficient time to his profession to become the highest paid lawyer practising before the Supreme Court.

The top point of his career, however, was his service to the Confederacy. First as Attorney-General and then as Secretary of War, he stood out as the most potent adviser of Jefferson Davis. At last, he was made Secretary of State and performed valiantly as Prime Minister of the Lost Cause. History has rewarded him with the familiar title "The Brains of the Confederacy."

He had pinned all on the Southern chance for success, and the conclusion of the war found his once great fortune swept away. Escaping after many hardships to England, he bravely set out to carve a new name for himself. Resuming his old profession, he speedily gained a reputation at the British bar. By writing the still famous "Benjamin, on Sales" he laid the foundations of a new fortune. Ten years after his arrival in London saw him Queen's counsel and a revered leader of the great English Bar.

He passed away peacefully in Paris at the end of his seventy-second year. They buried him there in Père la Chaise cemetery, where rest so many distinguished sons of France; and few indeed are the pil-

PREFACE

grims from America who have found their way to his tomb. His brilliant achievements, his fascinating personality, almost his very existence seem to have been forgotten.

If this volume shall in any way help to restore Judah P. Benjamin to the minds of his countrymen, it will be fulfilling the earnest hopes of its author. All the bitterness that followed the War between the States has long since melted into obscurity. North and South alike take pride in the accomplishments of all the great leaders produced by the historic controversy. Every American thrills at the brave tales of the Day of the Confederacy. And when he recalls the spirit of Calhoun, borne onward by the Sword of Robert E. Lee, let him not forget the indomitable Benjamin, gallant statesman of the Lost Cause.

"Judah P. Benjamin, the dapper Jew,
Seal-sleek, black-eyed, lawyer, and epicure,
Able, well-hated, face alive with life,
Looked round the Council-chamber with the slight
Perpetual smile he held before himself
Continually like a silk-ribbed fan.

. . . .

...The mind behind the silk-ribbed fan
Was a dark prince, clothed in an Eastern stuff,
Whose brown hands cupped about a crystal egg
That filmed with colored cloud. The eyes stared, searching."

John Brown's Body—STEPHEN VINCENT BENÉT.

Copyright, 1927, 1928, by Stephen Vincent Benét.
Reprinted by permission of the Author.

CONTENTS

☆

CHAPTER		PAGE
I.	IN THE SPIRIT OF SECESSION	19
II.	THE EARLY YEARS	
	1. Background and Youth	25
	2. At Yale	30
III.	THE EVOLUTION OF A SOUTHERN LEADER	
	1. Lawyer	40
	2. Planter	57
	3. Politician	63
IV.	THE SENATOR FROM LOUISIANA	
	1. The Tehuantepec Co.	74
	2. The Southern Bloc	94
V.	THE LAST DAYS IN WASHINGTON	107
VI.	"THE BRAINS OF THE CONFEDERACY"	
	1. Attorney-General and Secretary of War	117
	2. The Tragedy of Roanoke Island	132
	3. Secretary of State	135
VII.	"THE PREMIER OF THE LOST CAUSE"	
	1. Diplomatic Maneuvering	138
	2. The Ebb of Southern Fortune	154
	3. The Fall of Richmond	159
VIII.	TRANSPLANTED GENIUS AND RECOVERED FORTUNE	
	1. The Escape and the New Home	162
	2. Rebuilding Fame and Fortune	168
	3. A Leader of the British Bar	173
IX.	THE PEACEFUL END	183
	INDEX	201

ILLUSTRATIONS

"The PREMIER OF THE LOST CAUSE" *Frontispiece*

                                                                     PAGE

BELLE CHASSE PLANTATION   60
   From the drawing by G. F. Castleden, in the possession of the author.

THE SENATOR FROM LOUISIANA   96

RICHMOND HOME OF THE CONFEDERATE
   CABINET MINISTER   122

AN ILLUSTRATION OF BENJAMIN'S OFFICIAL
   CORRESPONDENCE   144
   This letter, in the possession of the Confederate White House at Richmond, is one of very few in existence. The Secretary burned nearly all of his correspondence before leaving the capital.

CONFEDERATE CHIEFTAINS   156

JUDAH P. BENJAMIN
Statesman of the Lost Cause

CHAPTER I

IN THE SPIRIT OF SECESSION

"THE chair recognizes the Senator from Louisiana."

The familiar, well-groomed figure attracted every eye as it took up a simple position between two desks, one foot crossed over the other. A death-like stillness stole over the packed galleries and even the buzzing voices ceased on the floor of the Senate Chamber. It was the last day of the year 1860 and Washington was tense.

Expounding on his favorite theme of Southern rights, with a dazzling brilliance of reasoning and a withering force of sarcasm, Judah P. Benjamin launched his attack:

"From the time that this people declared its independence of Great Britain, the right of the people to self-government in its fullest and broadest extent has been a cardinal principle of American liberty. None deny it. And, in that right, to use the language of the Declaration itself, is included the right, whenever a form of government becomes destructive of their interests or safety 'to alter or to abolish it, and to institute a new government, laying its foundation on such principles and organizing its powers in such form as to them shall seem most likely to effect their safety and happiness.'"

But quite aside from the right of revolution, there is, he went on, a right of secession. With force and lucidity he marshalled the historical and constitutional arguments in support of this idea, then asserting that "Even granting South Carolina has no right to secede, it is, nevertheless, a fact that she has seceded. You still have the same issue to meet face to face. You must permit her to withdraw in peace, or you must declare war. That is, you must coerce the State itself or you must permit her to depart in peace. It is absurd to attempt enforcing any kind of federal law in South Carolina. Where will you get a jury that will recognize your jurisdiction, much less one that will convict, in a community that has almost unanimously repudiated all connection with you? ..."

His manner continued self-possessed and resolute as he went over the whole ground of Southern causes of complaint. There was no fine speaking; no appeal as yet to the emotions; it was the cool and dispassionate reasoning of the Supreme Court lawyer; and yet the attention of the galleries was unbroken. He summed up his argument very carefully, read from a written paper in a measured legal tone the causes of difference, and then concluded. This conclusion was a telling shot, a magnificent, oratorical effort.

"And now, Senators, within a few weeks we part to meet as Senators in one common council chamber of the nation no more forever. We desire, we beseech you, let this parting be in peace. I conjure you to indulge in no vain delusion that duty, or conscience, interest or honor, imposes upon you the necessity of invading our states or shedding the blood of our people. You have no possible justification for it. I trust it is in no craven spirit, and with no sacrifice of the honor or dignity of my own state that I make this last appeal, but from far higher and nobler motives. If, however, it shall prove vain; if you are resolved to pervert the government framed by the fathers for the protection of our rights into an instrument for subjugating and enslaving us, then, appealing to the Supreme Judge of the Universe for the rectitude of our intentions, we must meet the issue that you force upon us as best becomes freemen defending all that is dear to man. What may be the fate of this horrible contest, no man can tell, none pretend to foresee; but this much I will say: the fortunes of war may be adverse to our arms; you may carry desolation into our peaceful land, and with torch and fire you may set our cities in flame; you may even emulate the atrocities of those, who in the War of the Revolution, hounded on the bloodthirsty savage to attack upon the defenseless frontier; you may, under the protection of your advancing armies, give shelter to the furious fanatics who desire, and profess to desire, nothing more than to add all the horrors of a servile insurrection to the calamities of a Civil War—you may do all this—and more, too, if more there be—but you can never subjugate us...."

The speaker paused a moment, one hand in his pocket, the other negligently toying with a vest chain. He balanced his head a little to and fro. Only his black eyes showed the emotion he felt. His characteristic faint smile, just a little scornful, appeared as he said, "But you can never subjugate us." He let go of his vest chain, and put his other hand coolly into his pocket. Half turning to take his seat, he added: "You never can convert the free sons of the soil into vassals, paying tribute to your power; and you never, never can degrade them to the level of an inferior and servile race! Never! Never!"

There was a moment of dreadful silence as the speaker slipped quietly into his chair—and then pandemonium. The galleries fairly shook with deafening bursts of applause, drowning out completely the buzzing voices on the floor below. The chair rapped and rapped for order—it was scarcely restored after what seemed like hours of effort. His face twitching with emotion, the presiding officer announced:

"A motion for adjournment is in order."

* * * * * * *

Several weeks passed. The exciting events of late December reached the columns of the London newspapers. They penetrated into the meetings of the British cabinet, where ministers eagerly reviewed the reports from Washington. "Have you read Benjamin's speech?" Sir George Lewis inquired of the Minister for Education. "Yes," replied Lord Sherbrooke. "It is even better than our own Benjamin [Disraeli] could have done."

CHAPTER II

THE EARLY YEARS

LIKE Disraeli, to whom he has been so often compared, Judah P. Benjamin was descended from Spanish Jews. Some acquaintance with that ancestry is the indispensable introduction to the man himself, as his life and personality reflected at every turn the experiences of his forefathers. To explain the one without a mention of the other would be impossible. Benjamin's greatness lay primarily in a peculiar ability to withstand the most harassing discouragements. Constantly recurring defeat was but the inciting force to the development of his genius. His talents were deeply rooted in the generations which had gone before.

His precursors lived in Spain for centuries during a time when the race to which they belonged filled the seats of the mighty. Culture and learning, pride and position, authority and active leadership, characterized the Sephardic communities. Their sons were found constantly in the front rank of the navigators, doctors, and brilliant scholars whose achievements were known throughout all Europe. Many of them, extensive landholders, bore the proud title "Grandee of Spain."

This is not the place to discuss the causes of the Inquisition. It came—that much is sufficient for our purposes, and in its wake followed the expulsion of the Jews from the Peninsula where they had lived and prospered since the early years of the Christian Era. The very ships which carried Columbus to the New World numbered in their crews a group of the unfortunates, including the chief surgeon and his assistant. As the *Santa Maria* cleared port, it passed other vessels filled with exiles and bound for places of refuge. Some of the emigrants settled in the Mediterranean World while others made their way northward to Holland. There, in the city of Amsterdam developed the community Rembrandt knew, from which sprang Spinoza, the philosopher. There, yet the interested traveller may wander about the ancient streets and hear strange names, so reminiscent of far-off Spain—Piza, Nunez, de Mendes, Castro, da Costa.

While Oliver Cromwell was dictating the affairs of state in England, a portion of this Amsterdam group received permission to cross the Channel and settle in London. Displaying the same genius for adaptability as they had on their arrival in Holland, these people soon adjusted to their British environment; they became an integral part of the great city which adopted them. To the original nucleus there was added from time to time other Spanish and Portuguese families, many, like that of the elder Benjamin d'Israeli, coming by way of Italy and the Levant. On the other hand fragments of the community would often drift away when some of the members left, to settle eventually in Brazil, Newport, Savannah, and the West Indies.

In the early years of the nineteenth century a recently married young couple left their London friends and relatives to shape their existence in the New World. The bridegroom was Philip Benjamin, a restless individual who might well have been the inspiration for the familiar adage about "A rolling stone." His wife, a member of the de Mendes family, was easily the stronger of the two, and the decision to leave England was undoubtedly hers. Several of her family had come to America and prospered; one brother-in-law was a wealthy planter in the West Indies, another a successful storekeeper in the Carolinas. If they could accomplish so much, why not her Philip also?

The island of Saint Thomas, then under the British flag, was the first American home of the Benjamins. And it was there, on August 6, 1811, that their second child was born. They called him Judah Philip. His life on the island was of short duration, for the family decided to move to the mainland while he was still a mere infant; restless and dissatisfied at his failure to make progress, the elder Benjamin was anxious for a change. The city of New Orleans, a growing center of trade, seemed a logical place to settle and preparations were made to sail there. When word reached Saint Thomas, however, that the city was being besieged by the British and the port was completely blockaded, the Benjamins altered their plans and

THE EARLY YEARS

took ship for the Carolinas. After a temporary stay in Wilmington, they established a permanent home in Charleston. Here Philip opened a small general store and here his young son first attended school.

Brilliant and ambitious, Judah quickly attracted attention in the small and prosperous community at Charleston. Moses Lopez, a leading merchant, took it upon himself to sponsor the boy's education and to urge his being prepared for college. It was finally arranged that he live with his aunt in Fayetteville and attend the Academy there. This was one of the oldest and best institutions of its kind in the South, having at the time of Benjamin's matriculation over two hundred pupils.

Under the special tutelage of a certain Rev. Colin McIver, the boy quickly gained a reputation. He was uniformly at the head of his class and was recognized as the leading intellect of Fayetteville Academy. Reserved in manner, he had few intimate associates while at school—and his time was chiefly devoted to work. A classmate said of him—"I never knew Benjamin to make an imperfect recitation, and the ease with which he mastered his studies was a marvel to every one."

From Fayetteville, he returned to Charleston, where his family was still located. Being people of quite some education and refinement, Judah's parents held their heads high, despite the continued low ebb of their fortunes. And Philip Benjamin now had seven children to support; besides Rebecca, the eldest, and Judah, there were two brothers, Solomon and Joseph, then Julia, Harriet, and Penina, the last born in 1824, when her brother was concluding his school days. On one occasion the prosperous relatives in the West Indies, suspecting the true state of affairs, sent generous chests of linens and other luxuries. Mrs. Benjamin returned them with thanks and the assurance that she was well provided for. But the less offensive assistance of those nearer at hand was not rejected; and to this the children owed their education. Moses Lopez continued his kindness to Judah and made it possible for him to enter Yale.

· · · · · · ·

It was the day of the orator and the embryonic statesman, when the forerunner of the blue jerseyed hero of the Yale Bowl earned his laurels at the rostrum of his debating society. Two great forensic clubs—with traditions reaching far back into the preceding century—flourished at Yale. They were known as "Linonia" and "The Brothers in Unity." To them a third society, "Calliope," had been added in 1819, as a result of the Southern students withdrawing from the two older groups. Sectionalism was already making its way felt and few indeed were the men from Dixie who could be induced to join the pro-northern clubs.

There were but two Southerners on the rolls of "The Brothers in Unity" when that organization convened for meeting in November, 1827. There was to be an open forum discussion of a problem uppermost in the political picture of the day. The subject was worded "Ought Missouri to have been admitted into the Union with the privilege of holding slaves?" Only a few years before Henry Clay had settled what threatened to be almost certain sectional strife with his "Missouri Compromise," resulting in Maine's entrance into the Union as a "free" state, balanced by Missouri's option to enter the "slave" group. Yale men were fanatically interested in the whole situation. Even the musty pages of the old minutes book covered with the story in scrawling long-hand fail to muffle the rabid enthusiasm of "The Brothers in Unity."

"All hammered away upon the negative until it got along up into the Junior class when one, after apologizing for not having prepared himself, had the *audacity* to say that Congress had no right to withhold this privilege. Mr. Mix alone, among all the others, *dared* to support this affirmative view."

Mix was one of the two Southerners then on the rolls of "The Brothers." The other was Judah P. Benjamin! Shortly after, both transferred to the "Calliopean Society."

Other topics that had been discussed by "The Brothers in Unity" during the year 1826-27 included "Ought the government of the United States take immediate measures for the manumission of the slaves of our Country?" and "Is it probable that our Country will continue under its present form of government for a century?" The issues discussed under these subjects were based largely on the questions of party interest, evils of slavery, sectional problems and the like. Both resolutions were decided overwhelmingly in the affirmative. And tho no record has been preserved as to just what members took which side, it is rather a safe guess that the greatly outvoted negative was stubbornly defended by the gentleman from Charleston.

Such observations may at first glance appear to have little significance. But remember that the undergraduate who had the audacity to defend States' Rights in 1827 was to be the Senator from Louisiana, who, thirty years later, would declaim the cause of the South thru the halls of a hostile Congress. The young man who learned to fight stubbornly and courteously for unpopular principles in his debating society would some day raise his head, in unruffled dignity, above a sea of disapproving confusion, to direct brilliantly the destinies of a Lost Cause.

As a sophomore Benjamin had won several honors in oratorical and scholastic fields. Speaking on the subject "Ought the United States to assist Greece in her present struggle for liberty?" he was a disputant at the annual "exhibition" of his debating club. His grades were among the highest in the class of 1829, being maintained at a consistent average of 3.3 (about 90 per cent) during his entire college career. Furthermore, he was awarded a Berkleian prize book, inscribed by President Day: "For excellence in Scholarship."

The years during which he was a student at Yale were marked by constant changes in the courses of study; the Faculty were striving for a reorganization and a greater systematizing of the curriculum. Now, there is no conservatism like that of students when they sense a change affecting what they suppose to be their rights. Accordingly there ensued numerous manifestations of open opposition on their part. They began to give expression to their feeling by petty and sometimes serious attempts to annoy those officers of the college who had particularly excited their indignation. The windows of these officers were broken, and their apartment doors were locked upon them.

In the attempts which were then made to put a stop to this mischief, it became necessary for the faculty to administer a severer discipline than had been usual. This only proved a new incentive to insubordination.

Some further action seemed to be called for. Accordingly as a convenient method of bringing their views before the public, the Corporation appointed a committee Sept. 11, 1827, for the purpose of taking into consideration the subject of altering the curriculum of study. This committee, as might have been expected, reported that, in its opinion, it was inexpedient to leave out of the courses the emphasis on the ancient languages—which was the fundamental cause of student disaffection.

Before the report could even be published a conflict had arisen within the walls of the college. There was at this time a large number of students from distant parts of the country. In the absence of facilities for speedy communications with their homes, they were peculiarly disposed to be carried away by gusts of passion. Whenever the student body gathered for meals at "commons," it became the regular habit to break plates and other crockery—as well as to toss the food out of the window. Every conceivable similar means of disturbance was invoked to demonstrate the general dissatisfaction of the student body.

Strict disciplinary measures were brought into action —and a number of expulsions resulted.

Such was the atmosphere that pervaded Yale in the fall of 1827. At the very end of December of that year,

Judah Benjamin, then a Junior, suddenly left college. His departure was evidently at the request of the faculty; but the exact circumstances seem destined to remain forever shrouded in mystery. The faculty records throw no light whatever upon the matter. Aside from the knowledge that he was unquestionably mixed up in the student riots, due to his general prominence in campus activities, there is only one specific clue. This is in the form of a letter written by Benjamin to the President of the College in January, 1828, requesting that he be allowed to return.

"Charleston, Jan. 14, 1828.

"Reverend Jeremiah Day.

"Highly Respected Sir:

"It is with shame and diffidence that I now address you, to solicit your forgiveness and interference with the faculty in my behalf and I beseech you, Sir, not to attribute my improper conduct to any design or intentional violation of the laws of the college, nor to suppose that I would be guilty of any premeditated disrespect to you or any member of the faculty. And I think, Sir, you will not consider it improper for me to express my hopes that my previous conduct in college was such as will not render it too presumptuous in me to hope that it will make a favorable impression upon yourself and the Faculty.

"Allow me, Sir, here also to express my gratitude to the faculty, for their kind indulgence to my father in regard to pecuniary affairs; and also to yourself and every individual member of the faculty for their attention and paternal care of me during the time I had the honor to be a member of the institution.

"With hopes of completing my education under your auspices, I remain, Sir, your most respectful and obedient servant,

(Signed) "J. P. BENJAMIN.

"P.S. May I solicit, Sir (if not too troublesome to you), the favor of a few lines in answer to this letter, that I may be able to judge of the possibility of my return to the University?

(Signed) "J. P. BENJAMIN."

There is no evidence that President Day even presented this letter to the faculty. Probably Benjamin and his roommate, John D. Boardman, were both involved in the ban, for the latter sent to the faculty a week prior to the date of Benjamin's letter, an apology, "for whatsoever was done by me, contrary to their laws or wishes, in the late affairs."

Benjamin's own statement on the matter, made

years later, obviously does not include the whole truth. "I left college," he said, "in the fall of 1827, in consequence of my father's reverses, rendering him unable to maintain me there any longer."

Just prior to the War, when political animosities overshadowed many a conscience, a newspaper article, purporting to come from a college classmate, went the rounds of the Northern press. It asserted that the needy young student at Yale had been both a desperate gambler and a thief. One night after he had gone to bed, said the writer, he had caught Benjamin going thru his pockets; to avoid exposure and expulsion the young man had left Yale.

Benjamin's letter of Jan. 14, 1828, quoted above, seems quite sufficient in itself to justify a dismissal of this story as entirely incongruous with the available facts and documents. As might be expected, he was incensed with the newspaper reports and even went so far as to hire Charles O'Conor and S. M. Barlow, northern lawyers, to run the libel to earth and prosecute those responsible for it. The editorial columns of his home town press were vigorous in their indignation. The *New Orleans Delta* asserted on March 2, 1861:—

"This is one of the vilest and most infamous attempts ever made to blacken the reputation of a public man whose great talents, astonishing energy, patriotic and dignified bearing in the public counsels have elicited the applause and admiration of the whole country. The story was hatched by Abolition malice, and the place and time of the incidents in it were selected with cunning regard to the difficulty of refutation.... This calumny has served to revive in the memories of all who are familiar with his remarkable career, the recollection of the innumerable instances of his generosity, his devotion to his relatives and friends, the prodigality, we may say, of his beneficence, and the remarkable absence of all sordidness in his whole nature and conduct."

The suit at libel became a practical impossibility, for two weeks after Benjamin was discussing it with his lawyers, Fort Sumter was under fire. Nevertheless, one may feel no qualms of conscience in utterly disregarding the slanderous propaganda. The picture of the brilliant young orator, the remarkable scholar, the courteous author of the petition to President Day does not in justice permit the mean embellishment given it by the violently hostile press of a later day.

CHAPTER III

THE EVOLUTION OF A SOUTHERN LEADER

HIS petition to reenter Yale having met with no success, Benjamin turned to the very practical problem of earning a livelihood. Proud and independent, he showed no intention of relying on his father for support; and that father was still finding it very difficult to achieve results with his small Charleston store. Early in 1828 the seventeen-year-old boy struck out for himself in an altogether new environment. After his three years at the stern, Puritanical college in New Haven, Benjamin entered into the most contrasting atmosphere imaginable—the romantic, bizarre, and convivial setting of by-gone New Orleans.

Passing along the streets today in the old French quarter, one can understand something of the easy sociability that used to transform the whole city into a single neighborhood. Courtyard doors all open, balcony touching balcony, terrace looking on to terrace —society was close, contiguous, continuous. What a cheerful picture of early morning warmth and sunshine is conjured up by the thought of those great courtyards, stretched open for all the breezes and all the world that chose to enter; the figs, pomegranates, bananas, crape myrtles, and oleanders, glittering in their dew; the calls in the street, musical negro cries, heralding vegetables, fruits, and sweets: "Belles des figues!" "Belles des figues!" "Bons petits calas!" "Tout chauds!" "Tout chauds!" "Confitures coco!" "Pralines, Pistaches!" "Pralines, Pacanes!"; the family marchande entering the courtyard swaying her body on her hips to balance the basket on her head. In the evening there was the promenade after dinner, on the tree-shaded levee, to enjoy the breeze blowing up from the Gulf and to meet with everybody one knew ... and see the constant wonder of more ships arriving....

Despite the heterogeneous manifestations of more recently intruded strata—American from the north, German, Irish—the nature of 1828 New Orleans was still fundamentally Creole. The architectural tendency continued to favor the Spanish type of massive brick houses, with their large courtyards—broad doorways—great windows—wide halls—palatial staircases enhanced by elaborate, fantastic hand wrought iron railings—and roofs resembling solid terraces, surrounded by stone balustrades. The city landmarks included the French Market; innumerable little coffee houses; the old Cafe des Emigrés, headquarters for the St. Domincans, where their favorite liquer "le petit gouave" was concocted; the Opera House with its tradition of brilliance and gayety; the grim Cabildo, where Spanish and French governors had once administered harsh decrees and imprisoned dissenting subjects. All these—features of a city on the Mississippi—were evidences of a spiritual allegiance to the Seine.

The English traveller, Buckingham, who visited New Orleans during this period wrote that below Canal Street everything reminded him of Paris: the lamps hanging from ropes across the streets, the women in gay aprons and caps, the language, the shops, particularly the millinery establishment on Royal and Toulouse Streets, "La Belle Creole," with its beautiful oil painted sign, representing a lady in *costume de bal* and another in *costume de promenade;* the winning persuasiveness of the shopkeepers; the style of living; the love of military display and the amusements, operas, concerts, ballets, balls, and masquerades without intermission from November to May; persons coming from theatre at midnight, remaining at masquerades until daylight.

The new culture, brought in by the thrifty, energetic Americans from the north, was just beginning to show signs of potential future predominance. North of Canal Street, in the Faubourg Ste. Marie, banks, newspapers, railroad companies multiplied, while commercial firms were springing up like mushrooms. Although the Creole element still maintained the upper hand in the general dictating of the city's life, evidences of growing strength in the "upstart" rival group were not lacking. This latter portion of the population was particularly active in the construction of the new wharves and in whatever else concerned the flourishing shipping trade of New Orleans.

Benjamin's first position was with one of the newly established commercial houses, where he worked for a short time as bookkeeper. Soon he associated himself with Mr. Greenbury R. Stringer, a notary, whom he served in the capacity of clerk. Under the almost paternal care of this kindly gentleman, the young man commenced to study law. In addition he determined to increase his fund of knowledge by becoming thoroughly familiar with French and Spanish. Though still a boy in years, he was shrewd enough to appreciate the advantages of such linguistic attainments if he were to follow any career whatever in New Orleans. And so in his spare hours he became a tutor in a number of different subjects. Whereas in some instances he received very welcome fees, for the most part he simply exchanged the teaching of English for that of French or Spanish.

With amazing adaptability, he grew into the ways of the Creole city, his deep emotional temperament reacting happily to the romantic setting. Small wonder then, the quick felt passion for his favorite pupil. The very spirit of New Orleans shone from her dancing eyes; the warm nights on the bayous were reflected in her languid manner. "Natalie St. Martin," he could not even say the name without a quiver of excitement running thru his entire being. She was the South he fell in love with.

His first visit to the home of Auguste St. Martin was as a tutor of English. His reward was to be the opportunity of learning French. And it was not long before his accent was excellent and his intonation superb—there were no words in the vocabulary of his mother tongue quite so adequate for his newly found purposes. "Ma chère Natalie—Ma bien aimée—Vos yeux sont ma Paradis...."

Strikingly beautiful and witty in conversation, the young lady dinted her French heels on a heart that, once aroused, would not be refused. She found her persistent suitor a most fascinating companion, sensitive to her changing moods and appreciative of her musical talents. His face would light up with enthusiastic joy whenever she consented to sing for him.

The lonely and yearning law student had found what he felt was the necessary complement to his existence—a companion of beauty, charm, and grace. And more too—for to him Natalie personified the environment with which he desired to harmonize and of which he hoped to become an important part; she stood for the permanence of Louisiana culture and life.

Too young to consider the matter from every angle, too emotional for a logical and reasoned understanding of marital problems, Benjamin quickly endowed his beloved with all the depth of companionship his nature required. The delicately nurtured blossom appeared to his passion-filled mind a sturdy perennial, prepared to weather every storm. It was an error only too common for young men in love.

Benjamin was called to the bar on Dec. 16, 1832, and a few months later Auguste St. Martin gave him the lovely Natalie in marriage. The young lady was a Creole, by which term is meant the child of pure-bred French or Spanish parents, born in a New World colony. Her family had emigrated from France to Santo Domingo and, during the "Black Horror," had fled thence to Louisiana. There was quite a colony in New Orleans of French refugees from the dark, turbulent anarchy that Toussaint L'Ouverture and the followers of Black Majesty had spread over the island of Haiti.

Despite her social grace and talent, the new Mrs. Benjamin failed from the first to prove an adequate companion for her husband. She was far more interested in brilliant society than domestic life. And she was a devout Catholic. Mr. Benjamin had been brought up a Jew, and was too proud of his hereditary religion, however slight the forms and practices of it upon him, ever to accept the Roman Catholic or any other creed. A marriage between persons of different faith is likely to prove unsound when neither party is sufficiently inclined toward compromise.

If ever there was a man who loved the home and knew how, even when preoccupied with affairs of pressing importance, to indulge in the little amenities that contribute so much to family life, that man was Judah P. Benjamin. Natalie in no way shared these simple domestic tastes; and tho he hid his unhappiness most scrupulously from the world, his married life was a keen and bitter disappointment. In fact, Mrs. Benjamin rarely figured at all in the events of his varied and colorful career. This tragic situation gave rise to frequent bursts of insatiable longing and a perpetual appreciation of irrevocable loss.

Their first home was in the city proper on Bourbon Street; but when her husband bought an interest in

"Belle Chasse Plantation," Mrs. Benjamin agreed to try life in the country. She found this decidedly uninteresting and dull, tho supplied with sufficient means to do all the entertaining she so much enjoyed. When the only child, Ninette, was four years old, her mother moved permanently to France, to educate her. The family was reunited only for a few short weeks each summer in Paris, where mother and daughter were established in luxurious style. During a period of adversity in later years, Mrs. Benjamin replied to one of his letters which cautioned her about expenses—"Don't talk to me about economy. It is so fatiguing."

Benjamin's powerful personality and indomitable will functioned best under conditions of adversity. The unhappiness of his marriage experiment served only to inspire greater concentration on a career—and the chance to forget which such concentration offered.

When he first began the practice of law, his principal problem was financial. In addition to taking care of his own family, he also contributed to the support of his mother and sisters. The New Orleans of that day, a busy and vigorously growing trade center, provided manifold opportunities for rapidly accumulated fortunes and quickly achieved reputations. However, even taking this into consideration, the young lawyer's rise was astonishing. His intriguing personality and tremendous energy brought him almost immediate recognition.

During the first year of his practice, Benjamin found sufficient leisure to prepare a valuable little treatise. Together with his friend Thomas Slidell (later Chief Justice of Louisiana), he drew up a "Digest of the Reported Decisions of the Supreme Courts in the Territory of Orleans and the State of Louisiana." It had originally been intended only for personal use, brief annotations accompanying the compilation of facts and analysis of the court's ruling in notable cases. When fellow lawyers began to borrow the manuscript, the authors decided that it had some real value; Mr. Slidell added more notes and some extra cases; the two then revised the treatise and published it in book form. It was considered accurate and useful enough to have a second printing within a few years.

The bar to which Benjamin had been admitted was

an exceedingly able one—and very large for a town of less than fifty thousand inhabitants. Among his contemporaries were the Slidells—Thomas, co-author with Benjamin of the "Digest," and John, of Mason and Slidell fame; Pierre Soulé, picturesque and fiery, some day to be minister at Madrid and to sign the startling Ostend Manifesto of 1854; Mazureau, greatest of the Creole lawyers; John K. Grymes, and numerous others, whose renown extended far beyond the American Courts of the old French Code. The Mississippi steamboats and later the railways brought a vast business to the thriving commercial center. And the wheels of commerce are generally the barometers of legal success.

In the field of Commercial law, Benjamin worked with an energy that seemed almost unbounded. From the very start he displayed the same painstaking attention to detail that characterized everything he did. Always armed with the concrete facts that this method supplied him, he was able to coordinate his quickness of apprehension, his faculty of logical presentation, and his masterful flow of oratory into a powerful and convincing attack. Of genius he betrayed every evidence; and to that native talent he added a vast fund of knowledge, built up under the moral drive of persistent effort. Perfectly balanced, perpetually in good humor, impossible to ruffle—his entire bearing invited the confidence of his clients.

Ten years of activity and success at the Louisiana bar prepared Benjamin for the famous case that was to make his name known far beyond the boundaries of his adopted state. In 1842 he became involved in the *Creole* dispute—a matter that dealt with international complications and provided room for a potential clash with England.

The brig *Creole*, flying the American flag, shipped a lot of negroes at Norfolk, Virginia, and set sail for New Orleans. While on the high seas, nineteen of the slaves mutinied, killed the agent of one of their owners, wounded the captain, and took command of the vessel. They ordered the crew to make for the British island of Nassau. On arrival there the mate jumped into the quarantine boat and soon after called upon the American consul to protect the ship. British officials took charge of the *Creole* and prevented the slaves from landing. The Attorney-General for the island investigated the mutiny and ordered the nineteen leaders to be held for murder. According to the American crew, the Attorney-General announced to the remaining negroes that they were free to go ashore and thus cast aside their status as slaves. The British contradicted this statement, insisting that the announcement in question was made by a passenger, and that the responsible officers of the vessel made no effort to hinder the landing.

The owners of the liberated slaves immediately instituted suits to recover damages. Judah P. Benjamin, with his associates, Thomas Slidell and F. B. Conrad, represented the insurance companies involved. The case took on the form of several suits—all of similar nature; the most important one, which served as a precedent for the others, was McCargo vs. The New Orleans Insurance Company. This was lost by Benjamin's client in the lower court, judgment for $18,400 being given against the underwriters. An appeal was made to the State Supreme Court, Benjamin preparing a brief characterized by its exhaustive consideration of the wider aspects of the case.

First he called attention to the clause:

"This policy covers all risks; and chiefly that of foreign interference. Warranted by the assured from elopement, *insurrection,* and natural death."

"Now," said Benjamin—

I. "The slaves owned by the plaintiff were embarked not at Norfolk but at Richmond, and the policy is only on slaves taken on at Norfolk.
II. "The insurors are discharged, the vessel not having been seaworthy. She was unseaworthy, in consequence of not being furnished with arms: from want of proper precautions and discipline with regard to the slaves.
III. "The occurrence of an insurrection of the slaves put an end to the risk. This was an occurrence against which the assured warranted the underwriters. On the breach of warranty the risk terminated.
IV. "The plaintiff's slaves were lost by the excepted risk: *insurrection.* The mutiny then was the proximate cause of the loss, even if a British interference to aid the slaves on their arrival at Nassau were clearly proved."

After a long succession of such technical arguments, supported by copious legal references, he introduced a more general and broad method of reasoning. "The insurance company is not liable," he asserted, "because the liberation of the slaves was not due to 'foreign interference' (covered in the policy), but to the force and effect of the law of nature and of nations on the relations of the parties. Against such law no insurance was or could be legally made." In order to substantiate this point, Mr. Benjamin had to present in some detail the status of slavery in the law of nations. He accomplished this by quoting the very passage of Roman law which he was later to discuss so feelingly in the Senate: "Slavery is against the law of nature; and although sanctioned by the law of nations, it is so sanctioned as a local or municipal institution, of binding force within the limit of the nation that chooses to establish it, and on the vessels of such nations on the high seas, but as having no force or binding effect beyond the jurisdiction of such nation."

Mr. Benjamin brought his case to a close with convincing eloquence: "View this matter as we may, it at last resolves itself into the simple question—does the law of nations make it the duty of Great Britain to refuse a refuge in her domains to fugitives from this country, whether black or white, free or slave? It would require great hardihood to maintain the affirmative as to whites; but the color of the fugitive can make no possible difference. It will scarcely be pretended that the presumption of our municipal law, that blacks are slaves, is to be made a rule of the law of nations; and, if not, in what manner are the British authorities to determine whether the blacks and whites reaching their ports on the same vessel, the former asserting their liberty, the latter denying the fact and claiming the blacks are slaves? It is obvious that the only criterion by which they can properly be governed is that which is insisted on by the American government, viz: if the blacks reach there under the control of the whites and as their slaves, so consider them; but if the blacks reach there uncontrolled by any master and apparently released from any restraint on the part of the whites, to consider them as free.

"These are the principles on which by the law of nations Great Britain has the right to regulate her conduct."

The final decision of the Louisiana Supreme Court was: "The Defendants are not liable on the policy in this case. It is therefore ordered that the judgment of the Commercial Court be reversed, and ours is for the defendant, with costs in both Courts." Benjamin had triumphed conclusively.

His brief was printed in pamphlet form and widely circulated. The young man who once excited his college debating club by having the *audacity* to defend slavery thus achieved his first public recognition in connection with that fundamental institution of Southern Civilization.

The large profits of his practice before the bar were not squandered, though generously expended. Much of it was used for the development of his "Belle Chasse" plantation, to which, in 1847, he moved his mother and sisters.

About this time he suffered a reverse that for a while plunged him into despondency, and ultimately led to his temporary retirement from the bar. The severity of the strain to which he had subjected his health, and particularly his eyesight, had not been realized in the high tide of success. Now, his eyes suddenly gave out, so that for some months he was utterly incapacitated for the practice of his profession. Depression followed —that depression which is so natural to energetic and ambitious temperaments when their progress seems blocked by entirely useless and incomprehensible checks. But the period of despondency did not last long. He resolved to relinquish his practice and give himself more assiduously to the fascinating occupation of cultivating sugar cane.

At this time the great Louisiana industry was still in its infancy. Many of the plantations in what is now the sugar and rice district were still devoted to the growing of cotton, though the soil was by no means well adapted to that plant. Furthermore where sugar was cultivated the methods were extremely crude. Few planters understood the absolute necessity of good drainage; few even understood the advantage of rotating the crops. And when the crop was grown, the methods of extraction and refining were unscientific, wasteful, thoroughly unsatisfactory.

Benjamin became interested in the subject just when some half dozen progressive planters were beginning to attempt improvements. He was by no means the pioneer, though he was among the earliest successful experimenters. Plunging into the theoretic side of the question with his usual enthusiasm, he quickly mastered the essentials of certain discoveries being made at the time by French chemists. His superior advantages, through foreign travel, knowledge of foreign languages, and naturally scientific habit of mind gave him an immediate preëminence among the Louisiana experimenters. Having tested the practical results of the discoveries, at "Belle Chasse," he proceeded to advocate the new methods in a series of papers, published in the once famous *De Bow's Review*.

For the great majority of their readers (and the periodical had a wide circulation), these essays first elevated the whole process, from the cane-field to the finished white sugar, into a science—and a highly profitable one. By thus popularizing useful scientific knowledge and contributing largely to the building up of a great industry, Benjamin well deserves high place in the agricultural history of the United States.

"Louisiana Sugar," the first of Benjamin's articles, contained a popular presentation of the improved process of manufacture, with tables of figures to show the practical results on plantations where the experiments had been made. There is also a very readable description of the apparatus of M. Rillieux, which

Benjamin had installed at "Belle Chasse": the juice was boiled in a series of "vacuum pans," always kept from contact with the air till it reached the point of granulation in the fourth and last pan—the evaporated steam from one pan being used to assist in boiling the syrup in the next. This system applied scientific principles to the problems of extracting a maximum of juice from the cane, filtering the juice to remove impurities, and economizing fuel by making use of steam in place of a direct flame for boiling.

Two years later Benjamin was asked to deliver an address on "Agriculture" before the Agricultural and Mechanic's Institute of Louisiana—but was unable to be in town at the time of the meeting. Consequently, at the Society's request, he sent his speech to *De Bow's Review*—and it was published as an additional article to his several essays on sugar. In this writing he quoted with pardonable pride from the report of Professor R. S. McCulloch, chemist for the Federal Government. This report described the efforts of Benjamin and Packwood (his partner in the "Belle Chasse" venture) to make chemically pure sugar direct from the cane-juice, without the slow process of the contemporary refining methods. "The crystalline grain and snowy whiteness were equal to those of the best double-refined sugar of our northern refineries. To these two enterprising men must be awarded the merit of having first made directly from a vegetable juice, sugar of absolute chemical purity."

When Benjamin's mother passed away in the autumn of 1847, his widowed sister, Mrs. Levy, was installed as mistress of the household. Possessed of a wonderful intellect, wit, and charm of manner—she was her brother's greatly appreciated official hostess. "Belle Chasse" became the center of a most interesting group of transient guests. Among those who came frequently was M. Auguste St. Martin, Benjamin's father-in-law, a delightful old gentleman, who was forever telling thrilling stories of the horrors of the great West Indian Slave Insurrection. Another popular visitor was the wizened little chemist—Rillieux—generally the centre of an admiring group of planters, to whom he would explain the high points in sugar-chemistry and in the working of his apparatus.

His various business interests made it necessary for the master of "Belle Chasse" to spend considerable time

BELLE CHASSE PLANTATION

From the drawing by G. F. Castleden, in the possession of the author

in the city. However, he made it a point to come out to the plantation without fail each week-end. He would send word to his sister that he would be down on Friday afternoon with six or seven friends and that she should please have broiled chickens with plenty of butter—"You know how I like them." Then without further notice the river-boat would arrive with twenty guests, "J. P." with a guilty look on his face, and a lot of expensive delicacies purchased at the last moment so that there should be enough to go around.

Benjamin was always ready to enter into the pleasures of the younger people. His niece, just then entering womanhood, found him her most sympathetic confidant, and many a seemingly tragic situation was made easy for her after a stroll about the garden with the great lawyer. For young girls he had a great affection; he loved to test their wits playing "geography" and "quotation" games. There was nothing he enjoyed more than telling ghost stories, working carefully up to the awful catastrophe, and suddenly crying out "boo." When his youthful auditors shrieked with genuine horror, his delight was unbounded.

But the pleasant days at "Belle Chasse" were soon

ended. The Mississippi rose and overflowed its banks—and the plantation was partially submerged. The growing crop was completely destroyed. At about the same time a friend for whom Benjamin had endorsed a note of $60,000 failed to meet his obligation, and the endorser was called upon to pay. There was but one course open. The expensive home in the country could no longer be kept up. His eyes restored to good condition, Benjamin resumed his practice in New Orleans—and moved his family to a home in the city. He, himself, kept bachelor's quarters on Polymnia Street with his two friends, the Huntington brothers.

Thus ends the plantation episode of his varied career—in disappointment and financial trouble. But there was no check on his onward march. With undiminished zeal and hopefulness he set about rebuilding the shattered fortune. And the plantation experience must be regarded as a valuable one in the light of future events. While owner of "Belle Chasse," Benjamin had become a slaveholder with the resulting opportunity of observing the slave question in practical operation. His subsequent views of the economics of the slavery question would take their coloring from his own experience

—which had enlisted his head as well as his heart on the side of the planter—to whom emancipation conveyed the threat of financial ruin and the gravest social perils. Furthermore, the leisure afforded by the brief period of plantation life gave room for speculation on things other than legal. And the fascination of contemporary politics suddenly dawned on Judah P. Benjamin.

. . . .

In the old South, most politicians were lawyers; and conversely most lawyers were politicians. It is, therefore, not surprising to find Benjamin experiencing certain contacts with politics at a very early stage in his legal career. Prior to the "Belle Chasse" venture, he had taken a small part in local activities, occasionally making a noteworthy speech. He showed no inclination at this early stage, however, toward being a candidate for any sort of elective office.

Of the still vigorous Whig party, inspired by Webster and Clay, Mr. Benjamin was from the first a warm supporter; and no small share of the flashes of success that came to it in the last decade of its existence in Louisiana is attributable to his energy and sagacity.

This was a time of desperate struggle for the Whigs, threatened first by defeat at the hands of Jacksonian Democracy; then, menaced by the insidious "Native American" attacks; and, at last, choking to death in an effort to swallow the Fugitive Slave Law.

Louisiana had been rather consistent as a Whig state until about 1840, when the waves of Democracy began to mount steadily; only the most vigorous efforts could bring victory to the adherents of Webster and Clay. The Whigs were defeated at the local New Orleans elections in April, 1842, and as a result exerted particular endeavor for success during the state campaign in July. For the first time, Benjamin was a candidate, and—after some exciting preliminaries, which featured the characteristic mud-slinging of the period—was elected to the Lower House of the General Assembly.

As a legislator, he showed himself able and resourceful, though no measure of importance was considered during his term. The nation was just catching its breath between the great financial panics that marked the Jacksonian Era, and Louisiana was preparing to call a Constitutional Convention. The people of the state wanted a new body of fundamental laws that would in some way prevent "wild-cat banks" without throttling finance, and that would place sufficient limitations on the General Assembly to keep it from potential robbing of the electorate at large. There was also considerable demand for changing the voting and office-holding qualifications. Benjamin showed himself heartily in sympathy with this distrust of democracy for its representatives—and approved the calling of the Constitutional Convention.

He was soon put forward as a candidate for that meeting, and, in a communication to the *New Orleans Tropic* (June 25, 1844), he stated his views. After urging that the powers of the legislature be restricted in regard to the formation of certain kinds of corporations, he expressed some decidedly conservative ideas on state banks: "It is too late at the present day to question the right of the states to charter banks, although I must confess that the strong bearing of my mind has always been against the Constitutionality of the exercise of such power by the states. I have found it very difficult to reconcile the idea of the coexistence of such power with those confided by the Constitution of the U. S. to the general government of coining money, regulating its value, and regulating commerce; and with the prohibitions by which the states are prevented from coining money, emitting bills of credit, or making anything but gold and silver coin a tender in payment of debt.... I shall vote, if elected, to prohibit the legislature from confiding to any body of individuals the power of doing banking business as corporators unless such corporators be individually liable for the debts of the corporation to the whole extent of their fortunes."

The election resulted in the choice of Benjamin and his associate, Conrad, to be the representatives of New Orleans at the Convention. The first session was held at the little town of Jackson on August 5, 1844; but, after three weeks of futile wrangling between Whigs and Democrats, it was agreed that the meeting be adjourned and that the delegates reassemble in New Orleans for further discussion. When the Convention reopened, one of the important questions under debate was whether special qualifications should be imposed on candidates for important state offices. Benjamin was among the considerable minority who insisted that no man should be a representative who had not been four years a resident and citizen of Louisiana. His speech on this subject was remarkable for the prophetic warning it contained—a warning that people smiled at then, as the figment of an alarmist imagination.

"This state," argued Benjamin, "is peculiarly situated, and her position exacts some measures of prudent forethought, in order to shield her from assaults upon a *vulnerable* point. Her peculiar institutions are liable to attack, and it is to preclude the danger which menaces her that some measure, similar to the one under discussion, is deemed of vital importance. Where is the impropriety of protecting, by requiring residence, the institutions we have met to remodel and perfect? ... There is one subject that I approach with great reluctance. It is of vital importance to the Southern States, and should produce, at least, unanimity in our councils to avert a common danger. It is not the part of wisdom, however we may differ, to wrangle where the safety of all may be compromised. I would scorn to appeal to party considerations. A question may arise within a few months that will obliterate all party distinctions, when there will be neither Whigs nor Democrats; when the whole South will coalesce and form a single party, and that party will be for the protection of our hearths, of our families, of our homes. That man must be indeed blind not to perceive from whence the danger comes. The signs are pregnant with evil. The speck upon the horizon that at first was no bigger than a man's hand overshadows us, and there is not a breeze that blows which does not sound the tocsin of alarm. The light is shut out, and we should prepare ourselves to meet the contingency whenever it may come. Our organic law would be deficient if it did not guard us from the machinations of an insidious foe. The course of events within the last few months proves that we must rely upon ourselves and our Southern comrades to maintain our rights and cause them to be respected—and not upon the stipulations in the Federal compact. We must insist for ample security for those rights."

It is clear from the above speech that two years of experience in public life had enabled Benjamin to rise above mere Whig partisanship and to hold a broad view of the conditions affecting not only Louisiana but the whole South. In this particular instance his policy was for the specific safeguarding of Louisiana—but in the light of the entire Southern problem. He desired to insert into the Constitution of his adopted state every provision, however remote the application might appear, to preclude the possibility of her own *bona fide* citizens losing control of the government. From this time forth Benjamin would devote much of his talent as a debater to defend the exposition he first set forth, years earlier, at Yale: the slave was property, and that, therefore, enjoyment of this property must be insured to the owner; if the Federal government shall fail in the assurance of this protection, the South must rise to preserve its institutions.

Benjamin's references to the rising tide of Northern hostility must be viewed against the background of contemporary events and their possible connotations. In the year 1840, the North began to react powerfully to the events of the decade preceding—a decade characterized best by a mention of the "Gag Law" and all that unfortunate measure implied. The Liberty Party was formed, and, four years later, its presidential candidate (Birney) drew to himself sufficient strength to ruin Henry Clay. When Benjamin spoke with conviction of a probable impending crisis, he must have been mentally reviewing what was transpiring around Boston. Unquestionably he was quite familiar with a gentleman up there who was advocating "immediate, unconditional, uncompensated, and unconstitutional emancipation of the slaves." He doubtless realized that there were many others who "would not hesitate, who would not equivocate, and who would be heard." Small wonder then that the farsighted champion of Southern institutions should shift the scope of his speech from local to national problems.

On the many minor points of Benjamin's activities in the convention of 1844, nothing need be said here. In all essentials he lived up to the promises he had made before election; and where he deviated from them, he generally did so in behalf of some compromise, which would at least accomplish part of the desired end. His own party wholeheartedly endorsed his actions.

For six or seven years after 1845 he was mainly occupied with the "Belle Chasse" venture, and, later, with his renewed activity as a lawyer. Like nearly all Southerners he favored the war with Mexico—seeing in its successful outcome additional strength to the cause of the civilization he loved. He retained his political contacts during this period by being always ready with advice for his party and by occasional public orations.

Through these years Benjamin laid the foundation for his fame as an outstanding public speaker—earning much favorable comment from critical contemporaries. One of these remarked: "He is calm and courteous in manner, with a voice as musical as silver bells. To a marvelous lucidity of statement he adds a remarkable power of analysis. He generally succeeds, with the most merciless logic, in exposing the sophistry of those who oppose his views."

Even his more impersonal addresses were characterized by a wealth of semi-argumentative material. He was asked to speak before a gathering of New Orleans schools in 1845, and delivered an oration that is to be found still in many collections of famous American speeches. His subject was "Education, the Foundation Stone of Republican Government." In logical, penetrating fashion, he built his paragraphs around the observation of Montesquieu that "Virtue is the cornerstone of republican government—and that virtue should be interpreted in terms of loving one's country and its laws."

"What then," questioned the orator, "are the means by which to kindle this love of country into a steady and enduring flame, chaste, pure, and unquenchable as that which vestals for their goddess guarded? Your schools! Let the young girl of America be instructed in the history of her country; let her be told the story of the wives and mothers of the Revolution; of their devoted attachment to their country in the hour of its darkest peril.... Take the young boy of America and lead his mind back to the days of Washington. Let him contemplate the hero, the patriot, and the sage, when the battle's strife was over and the victory secured, calmly surrendering to his country's rulers the rank and station with which they had invested him.

"Nor is it here that the glorious results of your system of universal education for the people are to be arrested. The same wise Providence which has bestowed on the inhabitant of the New World that restless activity and enterprise which so peculiarly adapt him for extending man's physical domain over the boundless forests that still invite the ax of the pioneer, has also implanted in his breast a mind searching, inquisitive, and acute; a mind that is yet destined to invade the domain of science and take possession of her proudest citadels. Hitherto, the absence of some basis of primary instruction has caused that mind, in a great degree, to run riot, for want of proper direction to its energies; but its very excesses serve but to prove its native strength, as a noxious vegetation proves, by the rankness of its growth, the fertility of the soil when yet unsubdued by man. Let this basis be supplied, and instead of indulging in visionary schemes or submitting to the influence of the wildest fanaticism, instead of becoming the votary of a Mormon or a Miller—the freeman of America will seek other and nobler themes for the exercise of his intellect; other and purer fountains will furnish the living waters at which to slake his thirst for knowledge. The boundless field of the arts and sciences will be opened to his view. Then shall we have achieved the peaceful conquest of our second, our moral independence. Then shall we cease morally as well as physically to be the tributaries of the old world."

CHAPTER IV

THE SENATOR FROM LOUISIANA

WHEN Benjamin returned from his annual trip to Europe in the fall of 1851, he was more inclined than ever for a career in politics. Those few unsatisfactory months with Natalie served only to remind him once again of the great gap in his everyday life, and to increase his determination to fill the void with constant activity. He was accordingly delighted to learn that his friends had placed his name in nomination for the State Senate during his absence abroad. He was elected without serious difficulty. Simultaneously, people began to mention his name in connection with candidacy for the United States Senate. While this discussion was at its highest point, the New Orleans *Delta* published the following editorial:

THE SENATOR FROM LOUISIANA

"Benjamin is sagacious, possesses great tact, and would make a very brilliant, effective senator. His appearance in that body would startle the gossips at Washington. His boyish figure and girlish face—his gentle, innocent, ingenuous expression and manner—his sweet and beautifully modulated voice would render him decidedly the most unsenatorial figure in that body of gray heads and full-grown men. But, when he should arise in the Senate, and in the most modest and graceful manner proceed to pour forth a strain of the most fluent and beautifully expressed ideas, of the most subtle and ingenious arguments,—of the most compact and admirably arranged statements—casting a flood of light over the dryest and most abstruse subjects and carrying all minds and hearts with him by his resistless logic and insinuating elocution;—then would the old Senators stretch their eyes and mouths with wonder, whispering to one another, 'That's a devilish smart little fellow';—then would all the ladies declare, 'What a love of a man!—what a perfect Admirable Crichton,—so beautiful, yet so wise,—so gentle, yet so terrible in sarcasm,—so soft-toned, yet so vigorous in logic!' The politicians would join in the general wonderment, and give their decided opinion that he was a psychological, physiological, and intellectual phenomenon. But with all his genius, his universal talents, and eloquence, Mr. Benjamin will hardly be elected to the United States Senate, because he is too valuable and necessary a man in this state. He is the acknowledged leader of several great enterprises, in which our state and city have a greater interest than in being ably represented at Washington."

However, the prophecy of the *Delta* fell far short of fulfillment. The vote for Benjamin in the Whig caucus was tremendous. And in the actual election victory for the Whigs was a foregone conclusion—due to the clear majority held by that party in the General Assembly. The same newspaper quoted above accounted for the election by stating that—"The country members of the Legislature preferred a gentleman who was a sugar planter, and had, therefore, a common interest and sympathy with them." This appears to be the logical explanation of his having been chosen in preference to Duncan Kenner and Randell Hunt, his seniors in party service.

Since his term in the Senate of the United States did

not begin until March 4, 1853, he continued his activities in state politics. Still a member of the Louisiana Upper House, he took a prominent part, during the winter of 1852, in the general work of the legislature. Another Constitutional Convention was in the offing—and Benjamin made a strong fight to insure Whig control of that gathering. He was successful in this, and was himself chosen to head the New Orleans delegation.

The Convention met at Baton Rouge on July 5th. Though the changes it made were in many cases radical, it was not so important a body as that which met in 1845 and excited less popular interest. The previous gathering had taken five months to patch up the Constitution, and, in the last analysis, had made few changes; in 1852, a new Constitution was enacted in less than a month with at least a dozen capital changes. When such an amount of work was accomplished in that time, it is needless to remark that there was little debate; the ideal of the body was to do with precision and speed those things which the majority demanded. Benjamin was the directing spirit of this majority group, which, peculiarly enough, advocated the same liberal type of measures that their leader had opposed in the 1845 meeting.

Seven years before he had argued for life appointments in the case of Supreme Court Judges; now he led the fight for making these positions elective in nature and ten years' length in duration. His former decided conservatism was replaced by an equally definite liberal tendency. In 1845 the Convention had ordained that the governorship could be bestowed only on men above thirty-five and with a Louisiana residence record of at least fifteen years. At that time Mr. Benjamin felt such provisions to be insufficiently conservative. In 1852, he voted to set the age limit at twenty-eight, the residence at four years.

All these are sufficient in themselves to bring up the irrefutable charge of inconsistency. But in another series of provisions he went so much further in his inconsistencies that his enemies had ample opportunity to blame his change in attitude on purely selfish motives. At the previous Convention he had opposed "slave representation"; now he was its chief exponent. In 1845, he had been a lawyer owning no slaves, while in 1852 he was a sugar planter and large slave-owner.

Therefore, argued his enemies, Benjamin now advocates that the plantation owners be permitted additional representation on behalf of their slaves in order to secure for himself and his friends the greatest possible political advantages. The fact that most of the wealthy planter families of the state were Whigs—and that since 1845 Benjamin had developed into a very loyal "party man"—gives to this attitude a coloring of undeniable truth.

Nevertheless, his changed course of action would seem to rest primarily on foundations that go even deeper. He was clever enough not to cling with desperation to principles that were no longer "live issues"; he was ever willing to respond to the needs of the hour and shift with the shifting times. Accordingly, he had yielded with the majority of his party in Louisiana to the popular demand for liberal measures, though his own choice may have been quite different.

Judah P. Benjamin was a remarkable opportunist in the realm of method. Obdurate in his drive for an end, he was incredibly versatile in his employment of means. His objectives were those of a statesman and were shrouded in the idealism of a leader who would champion a much-cherished cause. But the steps toward that leadership were the carefully planned movements of the practical politician. Specific inconsistencies and particular selfish motives are not to be apologized for or furtively slipped into the background; rather, should they be regarded as the inevitable possessions of the political strategist driving toward what he considers a worth while condition of state.

The time soon arrived for Benjamin to take his place at Washington in the Senate of the United States. The Democratic Party in Louisiana tried to prevent his taking his seat in Congress by advancing arguments built around the rather thin contention that he had been illegally chosen; some further objection was raised on the grounds that he was a native of St. Thomas. Pierre Soulé, Senior Senator from Louisiana, presented the petition to the Upper House on behalf of his state party—and refused to comment on it; he was obviously entirely out of sympathy with this narrow partisan move of his constituents. There being no substantiating evidence or remarks, the petition was quickly tabled—and Benjamin took his seat.

Since he acted constantly and loyally with the dwindling Whig party during a Democratic Administration, he found little opportunity for a conspicuous share in lawmaking. However, he delivered a number of speeches which must have corroborated the reputation of a brilliant debater which he had brought with him to Washington.

While in the Capital, he kept carefully in touch with local affairs back in Louisiana. He had been compelled to abandon completely his sugar planting activities, but there were several other projects of great utility for his state which continued to occupy his attention. The most notable of these was the Tehuantepec Railroad.

The story of the Louisiana-Tehuantepec Company reveals one of the most fascinating episodes in Benjamin's entire career, for this ill-fated venture is staged against a background of magnificently fantastic dreams and of an almost oriental exuberance. The potentialities of trans-isthmian communication, made more realistic by the "gold rush" in California, had fired the imaginations of the general American population. The atmosphere was charged with ideas and predictions and statements about railways which soon were proved to be utterly fanciful and unwarranted. The difficulties of construction, of obtaining materials and equipment, and of remunerative operation were incomparably great; and yet intelligent men spoke of a railway across the almost unknown, unsurveyed wilds of Southern Mexico, as if they expected to make a journey on it the very next week.

A glance at the map is sufficient to reveal what lay behind the Tehuantepec Railroad scheme, which a prominent group of New Orleans citizens began to boom in the spring of 1850. There were two logical routes, geographically speaking, for communication between California and eastern United States: A great semicircle running through San Francisco, the Isthmus of Panama, and New York, was one; the second would be a considerably smaller curve, running through San Francisco, Tehuantepec, and New Orleans. Development of the former implied the flow of trade to New York from the West, while New Orleans would reap the benefits of that trade flow, in the event of the second route being made possible. In the light of these potential economic advantages, the enthusiasm of the Louisiana group, interested in the Tehuantepec project, is quite understandable. Their leader showed himself just a bit too gullible; with all his practical sense and experience, Benjamin was too ready to believe what he was very anxious to believe and rather apt to take on trust statements which he afterward discovered, by personal investigation, to be quite unreliable.

The powerful interests centered around New York began to make themselves felt in 1846, when the United States signed a treaty with New Granada (now the Colombian Republic) which made possible the building of an American railroad across the Isthmus of Panama. A few years later, Commodore Vanderbilt constructed such a railroad. The citizens of New Orleans, impressed by the advantages of the considerably shorter route across Tehuantepec and anxious to outdo their northern competitors, became active in 1851.

In order to understand the full significance of the Tehuantepec project, it is necessary to have some knowledge of the earlier attending circumstances.

On the first day of March, 1842, Santa Anna, President-Dictator of Mexico, issued a decree giving to Don José Garay, a Mexican citizen, the exclusive right to effect interoceanic communication across the Isthmus of Tehuantepec. The grant was very generous in its terms, permitting him to open a canal, or to build first a carriage road and then a railway. The grantee or his assigns were to have protection in all their rights as well as in their work, and the privilege of fixing tolls for fifty years on the canal or railway. All vacant land to the extent of ten leagues on both sides of the proposed route went to Garay. In return, he was to agree that the canal or railway was to be neutral; that the work on the line should begin within two years after the completion of the preliminary survey; and that any colonists introduced to people the land granted to him should become citizens of Mexico.

Garay had neither the means nor perhaps even the intention of undertaking the work on the railway himself. But the chronic disturbance in Mexican politics encouraged him to make a show of beginning, in the hope of obtaining further concessions. He did succeed in accomplishing this object, and from time to time secured extensions of the period of his grant. His fundamental object appeared to be speculation—pure and simple.

At the conclusion of the Mexican War, the American peace delegate, Trist, offered fifteen million dollars for the right of way across the Tehuantepec region. The Mexican commissioners replied, "Mexico cannot treat on this subject, because several years ago she made a grant to one of her own citizens, who has transferred his rights, by the authorization of the Mexican government, to English subjects, of whose rights Mexico cannot dispose." In this way Mexico indicated a positive recognition of the Garay grant, and of the transfer of that grant to Messrs. Mainning and Machintosh, a firm of English bankers in the City of Mexico.

Shortly after, Mr. P. A. Hargous, a Pennsylvanian with numerous Latin-American interests, bought the Tehuantepec rights from the English bankers. Like the two previous holders of the grant, Hargous had no intention of undertaking actual construction himself. He had obtained the rights by driving a shrewd bargain—and he was in a decidedly speculating mood. In 1850 he came to New Orleans and soon interested a dozen enterprising, wealthy citizens in Tehuantepec. The most conspicuous of these was Judah J. Benjamin, who almost invariably acted as spokesman and representative for the group. A temporary organization was formed with Benjamin as chairman.

This company, unlike the previous purchasers of the right of way across Tehuantepec, was really in earnest in its desire to avail itself of the privileges acquired. Mr. Benjamin firmly believed that the possession of a railway, with good harbors at each end, across the one hundred and sixty miles of Tehuantepec, would revolutionize the fast-growing California traffic; would give command of the trade of the East; would bring to New Orleans immense benefits. In a speech before the South-Western Railroad Convention, he exclaimed, "... and when we cross the Isthmus, this Isthmus of Tehuantepec—what have we before us? The Eastern World! Its commerce has been the bone of many a bloody contest. Its commerce makes empires of the countries to which it flows, and when they are deprived of it, they are as empty bags, useless, valueless. That commerce belongs to New Orleans."

Immediately after its organization, the Company

started to take steps to secure the rights it had obtained. Application was made to secure the protection of the United States and to ascertain "the honest intention of Mexico to forward the great enterprise." Webster, then Secretary of State, was favorably impressed. He instructed the Minister to Mexico, Mr. Letcher, to make overtures for a treaty giving joint protection to the works. The American proposals were favorably received by the Mexican President—who drew up a draft treaty, subject to ratification by the Senates of the respective states.

Negotiations were in process and the future looked bright—when rumors began to float into New Orleans implying that all was not safe in Mexico. A new President had come into office—Arista—and his attitude toward the Tehuantepec Company was extremely hostile. His first move was to force a bill through the Mexican Congress which was practically a complete abrogation of the Garay grant. The correspondent of the New Orleans *Delta*, in Tehuantepec, wrote to his paper in April, 1851—"There is no doubt that the Arista faction will destroy the grant."

In October, 1851, the New Orleans *Picayune* published a comprehensive editorial, which should be reproduced here.

"New Orleans loses tremendously by the non-opening of the Tehuantepec Railroad. A large part of the rich traffic now pouring into the gorged coffers of New York would flow inevitably to this port, if the grand project of a Tehuantepec Railroad were completed: and the recital of all that New York gains awakens the regrets of every reflecting citizen of New Orleans for the delays and obstructions which the conduct of Mexico, not to say the indifference of parties interested, have thrown in the way of an enterprise of such vast interest to our people and to the whole valley of the Mississippi. We are here within three days sail of the shortest, and by all odds the best route to California, from the Atlantic states; yet nobody travels on that route—many persons look upon it as permanently defeated by the faithlessness of the Mexican government; thus far our proximity to it has proved of no value except to raise vain expectations that are vexatiously postponed. If half only of the travel which seeks New York were led to this point, the effects would be well worth a grand and costly exertion.

"There is a powerful interest hostile to this enterprise. The rival routes are going ahead with a rush and their interests center on New York. It would be irrational to suppose that they do not exert as much influence as possible to retard and defeat our work, thus incidentally encouraging the bad faith of Mexico. Let not any coldness or negligence on our part assist our ill-wishers. The gentlemen of this city who have so disinterestedly exerted themselves in this matter have, we are told, not relaxed their exertions, nor lost confidence in the establishment of their rights. Let them be aided by every citizen, and by every means in his power, to redouble their exertions and strengthen their influence with those to whom the enterprise in its present state turns for efficient interposition.

"Mr. Benjamin will, we presume, soon be at Washington on his way from Europe; and though we have emphatic assurances of the friendly disposition of the government toward us, we hope he may be able, and be assisted from all quarters to hasten the action of the Executive in negotiations to obtain an explicit acknowledgement by Mexico of the just rights of our citizens, which have been so wantonly invaded.

"A late New York paper in treating of the Isthmian travel says there exists a very strong rivalry between the Panama and Nicaragua routes; but that so many obstacles have been thrown in the way of the Tehuantepec route that it is doubtful whether that will ever be heard of after the Panama Railroad is finished. This would be a very disagreeable conclusion to us if we believed the prophecy; but we are confident that it will turn out to be a great mistake. This is so much the shortest, best, and most economical route to and from California that no route can compete with it once it is put into operation. That it will be completed sooner or later we haven't the slightest doubt. Our anxiety is that exertion should not be relaxed to bring it about as soon as possible."

Benjamin kept up the fight for some time longer—but, as we view the matter from the vantage point of today, the Louisiana-Tehuantepec Company was doomed. There is a notice to be found in the New Orleans *Picayune,* dated April 8, 1852, according to which Benjamin formally reported the transfer of all the Garay grant rights to his company. There is evidence in the *Congressional Globe* that Benjamin carried the matter into the United States Senate, when he reached there in 1853. He sought unsuccessfully to make the matter an international question; and urged the government to recognize the just claims of his company by taking definite action.

Then suddenly the Tehuantepec scheme sank into oblivion—and, in a tangled, unsatisfactory state—dropped temporarily from the stage. Just as suddenly in the early summer of 1857, the old project rose up again. More satisfactory arrangements for the holders of the concession were being persistently sought—and President Buchanan had entered into a plan submitted by Benjamin.

A new Louisiana-Tehuantepec Company was chartered on July 30, 1857—headed by Emile La Sère and Judah P. Benjamin. Its purpose was to salvage the losses suffered by its predecessor and eventually to obtain the original hoped-for results. Beginning with liabilities of several million dollars, the future of the new company did not appear too bright.

Buchanan sent special instructions to Forsyth, United States Minister to Mexico, informing him that Benjamin and La Sère were coming to him on a mission approved by the President; that they were to be formally presented to the Mexican Chief Executive; that their mission was not official, but on private business. Forsyth was to endeavor to secure from the Mexican government proper safeguards for the interests of the United States in any transit across Tehuantepec.

The American Minister resented the intrusion of the agents of the Tehuantepec Company, who soon after arrived in the Mexican capital. Although he refused to assist them, Benjamin and La Sère arranged a private contract with the Mexican government which gave a temporary assurance to the hopes of their business associates.

A brief season of prosperity came to the Tehuantepec Company. Mr. Benjamin raised funds and actually got built a practical road for vehicles across the Isthmus. He even coaxed a reluctant Postmaster General into granting a contract to carry the California mails via Tehuantepec for one year, commencing November 1, 1858. There was great jollification and congratulation. The mail came through from California, on the first trip, twelve days less than by any other route.

But it was all temporary, for this momentary covering of prosperity was but a thin veneer over a general condition of financial instability. The Louisiana-Tehuantepec Company was actually floundering in a sea of liabilities. Benjamin wasted the summer of 1859 in a vain effort to obtain financial aid from Europe.

McClane, Forsyth's successor in Mexico, was instructed to discuss the question with Juarez, who was then in control of the government. These last hopes, which appear so vain to us in this day, lingered on—until completely forgotten in the excitement over the election of Abraham Lincoln.

The explanation of Benjamin's connection with the Tehuantepec Company involves analyzing a series of complex motives and emotional conditions. The scheme appealed both to his reason and to his imagination.

There can be but little doubt attached to the contention that the Senator from Louisiana was a man of great civic pride, devoted to his adopted home and anxious to promote its prosperity. That he was not adverse to achieving personal advantages at the same time is equally undeniable. And that he saw opportunity for a potential source of great wealth to himself in the Tehuantepec Company seems quite apparent. Nevertheless, his conduct leaves the impression of irreproachable honesty.

That the project appealed to his imagination is also very evident. There is something almost reminiscent of Napoleon in his speeches about "the wealth of Empires," and "the Commerce of the Eastern World." In fact, Benjamin allowed his emotions to exercise far too much control over his reason throughout the entire undertaking. This fact, combined with Mexican irresponsibility and the power of rival American interests, accounts for the failure of the Company.

The significance of Benjamin's part in the enterprise is the indication of his remarkable versatility, his unbounded energy and enthusiasm, his true greatness of vision, which could survey the problems of nations with the same ease that it viewed the relations of plaintiffs and defendants.

. . . . . .

There have been few times in the history of the United States when the Senate personnel was more distinguished than in the decade prior to the Civil War. The spirit of the times was such as to tax every section of the country for the ablest leadership available; local electorates sought vigorously after the most powerful representation they might secure for the expression of their seething and wrought emotions. The versatile and brilliant debater was at a premium; and the Senate chamber constantly rang with the masterful oratory of Wade, Chase, Seward, Sumner, Everett, Douglas, and others in the shining galaxy. While paying tribute to his senatorial colleagues of the day, Charles Sumner asserted that he considered the gentleman from Louisiana to be the most brilliant orator in the United States. Dennis Murphy, official reporter of the Senate for forty years, described Judah P. Benjamin as the ablest and best equipped Senator he had ever known. Senator Vest asserted that he had never met the Louisianan's equal as an accomplished, well equipped, ready debater and legislator.

James G. Blaine, however, in his "Twenty Years in Congress," has most aptly summarized Benjamin's ante-bellum political activities, describing him as the author of the doctrine that the Federal Government is called upon to protect slave property. Almost all of Benjamin's important political speeches, from his advent in the Senate on, were directly concerned with this question. His first great lawsuit, the *"Creole Case,"* became a "cause célèbre" because of its relation to this problem; that was years before in 1842. The tendency toward emphasis on the same general matter is apparent in his Senate speech on the Kansas-Nebraska Bill, May 25, 1854—an exertion concerning which his chief opponent, General Cass, remarked: "I listened to him, as did the Senate, with the deepest interest. I have rarely witnessed, in my Congressional experience, an effort marked with higher powers of oratory."

Some time later, on February 23, 1855, Benjamin referred to a recently proposed suggestion that the Southern States withdraw from the Union, contending that the North was forcing the South into this position. After expressing the hope that he would not be in his Senatorial seat at that time, he went on—"I hope to take no part in such scenes. I hope to assist in averting that last lamentable catastrophe to the remotest possible time, but, sir, every day I am more and more persuaded it is becoming inevitable, and unless that kind Providence which has hitherto watched over our institutions with paternal care, unless that Power which guided our fathers in the Revolution, shall now guide and inspire us with wise counsels, breathe into us the spirit of peace and good will, and above all, govern and guide the conduct of

THE SENATOR FROM LOUISIANA

the people of the North, of our sister states, as we are still happy and proud to call them; unless this shall be the case, good-bye to this glorious Union of States; good-bye to all hopes of the successful attempt of mankind at self-government; the last, the great, the decisive experiment, will have failed."

On May 2, 1856, he delivered an address in the Senate on the Bill for the Admission of Kansas, in which he was the adversary of Seward. The hall rang with applause as the Senator from Louisiana with that cynical smile, which always accompanied his biting sarcasm, quietly remarked: "Strange, strange, sir, that that section of the Union which bears throughout the country the reputation of being so excitable, so passionate, so violent, is always ready to submit its claims to the decisions of the tribunals of the country; while that which is called the calm, quiet, calculating North, always obeying the law, always subservient to the behests of the Constitution, whenever this question of slavery arises—and this alone—appeals to Sharpe's rifles instead of courts of justice."

In the latter part of this same speech Benjamin explained the circumstances of his change in party affiliations. He had been elected to the Senate, originally, on the Whig ticket. With the decline of the party of Webster and Clay, he had switched to the Democratic ranks—and his reëlection would take place under the banner of his newly adopted organization. "And now, sir, when this struggle is narrowed down to a contest between the Democratic and Republican parties, I should be recreant to my trust—recreant to every principle of duty and feeling of patriotism—if I allowed my conduct to be influenced by the memory of past party ties, or past party prejudices. On that question whose paramount importance overshadows all others, the Democratic platform is identical with that of the old Whig party; and in declaring my adhesion to the former, I but change name, not principle. I, sir, therefore declare my purpose to join the Democratic Party. I declare my intention to use the utmost efforts of my feeble abilities to insure its success. In its triumph—as triumph it assuredly will—the constitution of our country will be secured from the dangers with which it is menaced; kind and brotherly feelings amongst the peoples of all sections of the confederacy will be restored; religious intolerance will be rebuked;

the equality of the States, the keystone of the arch of the governmental fabric, will be preserved intact; and peace, prosperity, and happiness will smile upon the land."

Beyond question, Benjamin's greatest senatorial triumph was his masterful reply to Seward on the Dred Scott decision, during March, 1858. Concerning this, J. L. M. Curry, one of his most scholarly contemporaries, wrote: "Benjamin's magnificent speech in the Senate in reply to Seward on the Dred Scott decision, was a masterpiece of polemic discussion, and placed him in the foremost rank of the parliamentary orators of our time. Calm and courteous in manner, with a voice as musical as silver bells, with marvelous lucidity of statement and power of analysis, with minutest acquaintance with every detail of facts and principles, with merciless logic exposing sophistry; in precise and guarded language charging misrepresentation, evasion, and perversion, every sentence a rapier thrust, bringing blood; holding auditors, friend and foe, in breathless attention, he added a new lustre to the great council chamber, which for fifty years has been the theatre of oratory and statesmanship."

How strangely prophetic—and yet, in the light of future events—how altogether logical that this period of ante-bellum activity should bring to the fore the names of Seward and Benjamin. There they were, in 1858, violently opposing one another, as Senators of the United States; and five years later would find them in a far bitterer state of opposition, with one holding the portfolio of Lincoln's Secretary of State—and the other at the helm of the "Lost Cause."

Early in March, 1858, Senator Seward of New York—expressing the disgust of his constituents and fellow northerners in general at the pro-Southern Dred Scott decision—made a bitter attack upon the Supreme Court and particularly upon the "obiter dictum" of Chief Justice Taney. To this attack the Senator from Louisiana replied:

> "In the exquisitely decorous language of the Senator from New York, the Chief Justice and the Chief Magistrate of the Union were gambling at cards for the case—and Dred Scott was dummy in the imaginary game.
>
> "Mr. President, accursed, thrice accursed, is that fell

spirit of party which desecrates the noblest sentiments of the human heart; which, in the accomplishment of its unholy purposes, hesitates at no reckless violence of assault on all that is held sacred by the wise and good. It was difficult, extremely difficult for all of us to sit here and hear what was said, and observe the manner in which it was said, and repress the utterance of the indignation that boiled up within us. All this is charged by the Senator without the proof of a solitary fact. Luckily, sir, luckily for us, these eminent men are too highly placed in the reverence and regard of the American people to have their bright escutcheon injured by such attacks as these. Mr. President, in olden times a viper gnawed a file."

Two days later, on March 13, Senator Wade, while attempting to refute Benjamin's speech, asserted: "I know that the honorable Senator from Louisiana, with that plausible and beautiful style of which he is so completely master, escaped from the rugged inconsistencies of this nefarious Dred Scott decision by passing a eulogy on the old Chief Justice. It was beautiful; it relieved him from the burden of encountering the enormous glaring unconstitutionalities and breaches of law summed up there. Why, sir, he went so far as to send the old man to Heaven even before he died!"

Not long after the Dred Scott debates and during the course of one of Benjamin's speeches, Jefferson Davis of Mississippi corrected a statement in an ill-natured manner. Whereupon Mr. Benjamin quietly repeated his statement in another form. Mr. Davis, who was in bad health and irritable, said he considered it "an attempt to misrepresent a very plain remark." Mr. Benjamin sat down at his desk, wrote a note of challenge, according to the prevailing practice of the day, which was delivered by the hand of Mr. Benjamin's friend, Mr. Bayard. Mr. Davis promptly tore up the note, said to Senator Bayard that he was wholly wrong, walked back onto the floor, made the most distinct withdrawal of what he had said, and regretted most amply any offense. Senator Benjamin rose and stated that he had been hurt by the asperity in the voice and manner of one whom he respected and admired, but that he would be very glad to forget all between them, "except the pleasant passage of this morning." Thus the incident was closed in a manner creditable to both parties. The statement has been made that Mr. Davis, a West Point graduate and a soldier of proven courage in the Mexican War, was so impressed with the pluck of the "little man from Louisiana" that this episode contributed much to what later became a fast and enduring friendship.

. . . .

In 1849, the New Orleans legal firm of Micou and Benjamin had been formed. Upon Mr. Micou's death five years later, it was succeeded by the firm of Benjamin, Bradford, and Finney, which continued during the remainder of Mr. Benjamin's service in the United States Senate and until the outbreak of the Civil War. Mr. Benjamin turned his salary as United States Senator into this firm, the annual income of which was said to be more than $75,000. It was divided among the partners in the ratio of five, five, and two.

During this period, Benjamin was selected by the United States government to represent it before the California Land Commissioners, for which he received a fee of $50,000—the largest amount ever paid to an American lawyer for a single case, up to that time. He was peculiarly fitted for this employment not only because of his legal talents, but because of his knowledge of Spanish.

On another occasion he was summoned all the way from Washington to South America, there to argue a claim in the Courts of Ecuador. General Villamil, who had been a resident of New Orleans, and had also been Minister from Ecuador at Washington, had purchased a claim to St. Charles Island, one of the Galapagos group located about five hundred miles off the coast of the small South American Republic. The General's title was not altogether clear—and, as the island was said to contain very rich deposits of guano—he was anxious to have his claim well handled. Benjamin went to Quito, the capital of Ecuador, and there successfully argued Villamil's claim in the courts—a remarkable and romantic testimony to his familiarity with the language of the country.

In 1851, upon directions from Washington, the United States Attorney at New Orleans retained Mr. Benjamin to prosecute General Henderson and other Cuban filibusters. Feeling ran high. Governor Quitman of Mississippi, himself a filibuster, spread the report that Benjamin had been retained by the Spanish government for a fee of $25,000. This poisoned dart, coupled with overwhelming enthusiasm for the downtrodden Cubans, made conviction impossible.

At the October term, 1848, Mr. Benjamin had been admitted to practice before the Supreme Court of the United States, but his first actual appearance there was in 1852. He appeared in nine of the cases reported in 59 U. S. At the December term, 1856, he won six out of the eight cases argued by him. He appeared in ten cases reported in 61 U. S.; and he won seven of his ten cases, reported in Volume 63.

One of his most interesting cases was McDonogh's Executors, where he and Reverdy Johnson, representing heirs at law, tried to break the McDonogh will leaving enormous legacies to the cities of Baltimore and New Orleans. Though Benjamin was for the losing side, the court notes the great power and ability of his argument. Glowing press descriptions appeared at the time. The reporter for the Washington *Union* enthusiastically said:

> "Who ever was not in the Supreme Court this morning missed hearing one of the finest forensic speakers in the United States. In the case of the great McDonogh

estate, Mr. Benjamin made one of the most truly elegant and eloquent speeches that it was ever my good fortune to hear."

In 1860, the last year of his American practice, he was engaged in California in heavy litigation over quicksilver mines. The case was appealed, but the War supervening, he was necessarily absent and could not argue it. In 1863, when Benjamin was in Richmond as "prime minister" of the enemy cause, his associates, A. C. Peachey, Reverdy Johnson, Charles O'Conor, and J. J. Crittenden, did him the signal honor of filing his brief before the Supreme Court of the United States.

Soon after he had taken his seat in the Senate, in 1853, Benjamin had been offered a place on the Supreme Court Bench by President Pierce; but the gentleman from Louisiana—anxious to retain all his varied political, legal, and commercial activities—respectfully refused.

CHAPTER V

THE LAST DAYS IN WASHINGTON

THE story of the year 1860 in American History is the account of a problem in applied psychology. Definite types of men moulded by the conditions of the times were the determining factors—not the slavery question in itself; not, primarily, economic forces; not a theory of government, nor a clash of theories; not any one thing; but the fluid changeful forces of human nature, battling with circumstances and expressing themselves in the fashion of men's minds. To say this is to acknowledge the fatefulness of sheer feeling. Jefferson Davis described the situation exactly when he said, during that year, "A sectional hostility has been substituted for a general fraternity." To his own question, "Where is the remedy?" he gave the answer, "In the hearts of the people." There, after all, is the conclusion of the whole matter. The strife between North and South had ceased to be a thing of the head; it had become a thing of the heart.

That a Secession movement would begin somewhere in the South before the end of 1860 was a foregone conclusion. South Carolina was the logical place, and in South Carolina the inevitable occurred. The presidential election, which had brought victory to the "Black Republican," was quickly followed by an election of delegates, on the 6th of December, to consider in convention the relations of the State with the Union. In a burst of passionate zeal the independence of South Carolina was proclaimed on December 20, 1860, by an ordinance of secession.

During the eight days that followed, Washington was in a state of confused helplessness. President Buchanan, vacillating and nervously evasive, refused to declare either for the Southern position or against the right of Secession. In the words of Senator Seward, "Buchanan showed conclusively that it is the duty of the President to execute the laws—unless somebody opposes him; and that no State has a right to go out of the Union—unless it wants to."

On the 28th of the month, however, came a turning-point. Buchanan was just on the verge of turning over to Commissioners from South Carolina the forts and other federal property in their state; he even drew up a paper to that effect and showed it to the Cabinet. Black, Holt, and Stanton—his three most powerful advisers—threatened immediate resignation unless the paper should be destroyed. The President gave in and refused the demand for the surrender of the forts.

The reaction of this stronger northern position was felt immediately in the Senate. That dissolution of the Union was inevitable had been in every one's mind for some months; that this dissolution could never be peaceable was now becoming apparent. And on the last day of the year 1860, the Senator from Louisiana determined to make clear the actual, practical situation in South Carolina now that she had seceded; to establish the right of secession; and to show the wrong and folly of the course proposed by the administration.

He prefaced his remarks with a quiet allusion to the traditional American attitude on the right of self-government; and then burst into the brilliant onslaught of logic, described in the opening chapter. His eloquent peroration, we noted there, had a tremendous dramatic effect. Representatives of North and South alike, in the closely-packed galleries and on the floors of the Senate Chamber, broke up the meeting with uncontrollable applause.

Reading thru that magnificent speech of December 31st, 1860, we experience true contact not only with Benjamin the zealous champion of the Southern cause but with Benjamin the wily politician of far seeing vision. That the Senator from Louisiana spoke with sincerity and with a sense of passionate devotion to the cause he loved seems undeniable; that he was making a powerful bid for a position of leadership in the newly forming Confederacy seems equally beyond refutation. His talk was nominally directed toward the ears of the North—a plea to let "my people depart in peace." But in reality every phrase of that dramatic peroration was a passionate appeal to the emotions of the South. The party of Abraham Lincoln could never be persuaded by such arguments; irritation, rather than conciliation, must be their eventual plausible reaction. On the other hand, the thoroughly aroused public opinion of the Southland was bound to greet such words as Benjamin's with the enthusiastic conviction that here was a leader for their great purposes.

In order to understand fully, then, the true significance of Benjamin's powerful orations during this critical period, one must apply to them the formulas suggested above—sincere conviction and wily deliberation. These are points well worth keeping in mind as we turn our attention now to the farewell speech of the Gentleman from Louisiana, delivered on February 4th, 1861.

General E. D. Keyes, of the United States Army, was at the time a young officer in Washington, and used to visit Congress and report to General Scott the doings of the politicians. In his memoirs, he discusses the happenings of February 4th:

"... I heard the farewell speeches of Jefferson Davis of Mississippi and Benjamin of Louisiana. ... Mr. Benjamin appeared to be essentially different from Mr. Davis ... he never excited animosity in me or in any other Northern man so far as I am aware. When I listened to his last speech in the Senate, I was transported out of myself. Such verbal harmony I have never heard before! There was neither violence in his action nor anger in his tone, but a pathos that lulled my senses like an opiate that fills the mind with delightful illusions. I was conscious that it was Senator Benjamin who spoke, and that his themes were mighty wrongs and desperate remedies; but his words I could not recite, nor can I yet recall them. Memory, however, restores the illusive pleasure they left, which is like the impression I retain of my youthful days."

What an acid test of oratorical and debating genius! Saying things that constituted a fierce attack upon the honesty, fairness, honor of his opponents—and saying them in that piercingly melodious voice, without apparent passion and with all the arts that rhetoric could teach—Benjamin gave no offense, rather stirring his hostile listeners to mingled admiration and regret.

His main theme in this farewell speech is an explanation of the particular position of his home state—and his logic during the entire exposition is masterful:

"Sir, it has been urged on more than one occasion, in the discussions here and elsewhere, that Louisiana stands on an exceptional footing. It has been said that whatever may be the rights of the states that were original parties to the Constitution—even granting their right to resume, for sufficient cause, those restricted powers which they delegated to the general government in trust for their own use and benefit—still Louisiana can have no such right, because she was acquired by purchase. Gentlemen have not hesitated to speak of the sovereign states formed out of the territory ceded by France as property bought with the money of the United States, belonging to them as purchasers; and although they have not carried their doctrine to its legitimate results, I must conclude that they also mean to assert, on the same principle, *the right of selling for a price that which for a price was bought.*

"I shall not pause to comment on this repulsive dogma of a party which asserts the right of property in free-born white men, in order to reach its cherished object of destroying the right of property in slave-born black men; still less shall I detain the Senate in pointing out how shadowy the distinction between the condition of the servile African and that to which the white freemen of my state would be reduced, if it indeed be true that they are bound to this government by ties that cannot be legitimately dissevered, without the consent of that very majority which wields its powers for their oppression.

"I simply deny the fact on which the argument is founded. I deny that the province of Louisiana, or the people of Louisiana, were ever conveyed to the United States for a price, as property that could be bought or sold at will. Without entering into the details of the negotiation, the archives of our State Department show the facts to be, that although the domain, the public lands, and other property of France in the ceded province, were conveyed by absolute title to the United States, the sovereignty was not conveyed otherwise than in trust. What is the express language of the treaty?— 'The inhabitants of the ceded territory *shall be incorporated in the Union* of the United States and admitted as soon as possible, according to the principles of the Federal Constitution, to the enjoyment of *all* the rights, immunities, and privileges of citizens of the United States; and in the meantime they shall be maintained and *protected* in the enjoyment of their liberty, property, and the religion which they possess.'"

After further strengthening the already powerful defense of Louisiana's *right* to secede, the orator poured forth his final, stirring peroration:

"We are told that the South is in rebellion without cause, and that her citizens are traitors. Rebellion! The very word is a confession; an avowal of tyranny, outrage, and oppression. It is taken from the despot's code, and has no terror for other than slavish souls. When, sir, did millions of people, as a single man, rise in organized, deliberate, unimpassioned rebellion against justice, truth, and honor? Well did a great Englishman exclaim on a similar occasion: 'You might as well tell me that they rebelled against the light of heaven; that they rejected the fruits of the earth. Men do not war against their benefactors; they are not mad enough to repel the instincts of self-preservation. I pronounce fearlessly that no intelligent people ever rose, or ever will rise, against a sincere, rational, and benevolent authority. No people were ever born blind. Infatuation is not a law of human nature. When there is a revolt by a free people, with the common consent of all classes of society, there must be a *criminal* against whom that revolt is aimed.'

"Traitors! Treason! Ay, sir, the people of the South imitate and glory in just such treason as leaped in living flame from the impassioned lips of Henry; just such treason as encircles with a sacred halo the undying name of Washington."

The transition from the author of these sentiments to an executor of the plans they suggested was made comparatively easy for Benjamin by the enthusiasm with which he was received on his return South. He had left Washington for New Orleans, directly following his speech of February 4th—and his name was already being mentioned in Louisiana as a candidate for Vice Presidency of the Confederacy. However, he would not have been eligible, even if he had been willing to accept such an office, because of his foreign birth. And imagine a man of Benjamin's energy content to subside into a position of such hopeless inaction as that of the Vice President?

On February 26th the press announced Benjamin's nomination to be Attorney-General of the newly formed government—and shortly after, his personal affairs having been set in order, he left New Orleans for Montgomery.

He was soon to begin the greatest experience of his life. The more familiar one becomes with the story of the Confederacy and Benjamin's part in its gallant struggle, the more convinced he must become that this indeed was the high point in the man's career.

If John C. Calhoun was the Mazzini and Robert E. Lee the Garibaldi of the Lost Cause, then surely Judah P. Benjamin was its Cavour.

CHAPTER VI

"THE BRAINS OF THE CONFEDERACY"

JEFFERSON DAVIS has himself supplied us with the story of how the first Confederate Cabinet was formed. "After being inaugurated," he wrote, "I proceeded to the formation of my Cabinet, that is, the heads of the executive departments authorized by the laws of the Provisional Congress. The unanimity existing among our people made this a much easier and more agreeable task than where the rivalries in the party of an executive have to be consulted and accommodated, often at the expense of the highest capacity and fitness. Unencumbered by any other consideration than the public welfare, having no friends to reward or punish, it resulted that not one of those who formed my first Cabinet had borne to me the relationship of close personal friendship, or had political claims upon me; indeed, with two of them, I had no previous acquaintance."

Davis then proceeded to give brief explanations of his specific choices. In regard to his selection for Attorney-General, he said: "Mr. Benjamin, of Louisiana, had a very high reputation as a lawyer, and my acquaintance with him in the Senate had impressed me with the lucidity of his intellect, his systematic habits, and his capacity for labor. He was therefore invited to the post of Attorney-General."

With all his protestations, however, about picking his advisers solely because of merit, Davis did fall victim to a serious error in executive judgment. The men chosen were far from incapable; but it may be doubted if any of them really fitted the executive department over which he was called to preside at a time when only peculiar fitness and talent could achieve success. It is obvious that Davis based his selections primarily upon the desire to distribute the positions among the various seceded states and among the several factions in those states. Thus, a catering to certain political demands overshadowed the more pressing exigencies for specific, well placed talents. The composition

"THE BRAINS OF THE CONFEDERACY"

of the first cabinet, then, was somewhat unfortunate.

It was ridiculous to see a man of Benjamin's proven abilities wasting his time in the child's play of Attorney-General to a government that had scarcely any courts. Beyond giving occasional opinions to other executive officers, he was comparatively idle, so far as the duties of his own department were concerned. However, his shrewd opinions on matters pertaining to the War and State departments were quickly discovered, sought after, and listened to.

The position that Benjamin was to occupy in the Councils of the Confederate Government was clearly revealed in the first Cabinet meeting held at Montgomery. It was in a little room just off the parlor of the old Exchange Hotel that Jefferson Davis met with his recently selected advisers. This was several weeks before the firing on Sumter, and the majority of the Southern leaders were still laughing at the idea of serious fighting. Leroy P. Walker, Davis's Secretary of War, had just returned from a speaking tour through Alabama in which he had been promising to wipe up with a pocket handkerchief all the blood that would be shed to accomplish secession. Years afterwards this same Walker declared: "The only man who showed any sense at our first cabinet meeting was Mr. Benjamin."

The far-sighted Attorney-General was indeed the only man present who seemed to visualize a long-drawn-out struggle. In his brisk lively manner, he predicted that the independence of the South could be maintained only by a hard-won fight. Preparedness and immediate action formed the keynote of his attitude, as he vigorously put forward his proposals. "I recommend," he insisted, "that our government purchase, immediately, at least 100,000 bales of cotton and ship it to England. With the proceeds of a part of it, let us purchase 150,000 stand of small arms, together with a corresponding amount of guns and munitions. The residue of the cotton should be held as a basis for credit."

His colleagues ridiculed the idea of a long, difficult war—and the proposal was unheeded. Some weeks later when Sumter fell, and Abraham Lincoln issued his first call for volunteers, the cabinet realized too late that it had blundered. The short, stout man with the full face and the perpetual smile was accorded greater respect.

The Provisional Congress, in session at Montgomery, on the 21st of May, 1861, resolved "that this Congress will adjourn on Tuesday next, to meet again on the 20th day of July at Richmond, Virginia." The Old Dominion had seceded—and because of its geographical position, as well as its general importance, was the logical site for the Confederate capital.

While on his way north, the Attorney-General used his oratorical powers to excellent advantage. He addressed gatherings in many of the towns thru which he passed, promising that the Confederate Government would employ vigorous action to expel the invader. Arriving in Richmond, he took up his residence in the Davenport home on Main Street, between Adams and Fushee. His friends—Congressmen Kenner and Conrad from Louisiana—and his brother-in-law, Jules St. Martin, soon after joined his household. They lived there very modestly for the duration of the war.

The weeks after his arrival in the capital were filled with troop movements. Beyond the city limits rows of white tents grew up in ever increasing numbers. Bound up, heart and soul, in "The Cause," Benjamin thrilled at the stirring sights. No descendant of Virginia cavaliers could have felt himself more a part of the spirit of the South than its foreign-born cabinet minister. All that he had fought for during those long years in the Senate, all that he had cherished as his own beloved civilization, seemed blazoned across the banner that carried the Stars and Bars. He stood in silence beside his chief, the perpetual smile playing peculiarly about his mouth, as the Richmond Light Infantry Blues, on their way to the front, passed in review. The band was playing bravely and the heads of the young men were proud and erect. "The flower of the South," remarked Davis to those who stood about him; Benjamin scarcely heard him, his eyes following the direction of the "Bonnie Blue Flag" and his lips moving with the music:

"In Dixie land, I'll take my stand,
To live and die for Dixie."

Through these long weeks Benjamin had little to do in his capacity as Attorney-General. It soon became

Residence of Judah P. Benjamin

RICHMOND HOME OF THE CONFEDERATE CABINET MINISTER

"THE BRAINS OF THE CONFEDERACY"

evident that in the stress of war, the niceties of legal discrimination would be quickly swept aside. Accordingly, since his legal services were not in demand, he commenced to busy himself with other matters. Ever the wily diplomat, he had carefully studied the idiosyncrasies of Mr. Davis and was following a well-planned path toward winning favor. His urbanity and thorough realization of the proper relations of a cabinet officer to his chief quickly won the President's gratitude—particularly when compared with the insubordinate resentment shown by the other ministers to their chief's haughty, dictatorial methods. And his unusual abilities became more obvious than ever to Jefferson Davis.

During the summer he was a frequent visitor at the War Department. When the news reached there by telegraph that the South had triumphed on the battlefield of Manassas, it was Benjamin who repeated the inspiring news by memory to the anxious, crowding group of reporters. An eye-witness remarked that "his face glowed something like Daniel Webster's after taking a pint of brandy."

The battle of Manassas had proved to Secretary of

War Walker that his pocket handkerchief would be most insufficient to wipe up the blood which was destined to be shed. He found himself unequal to the strain produced by his constantly increasing duties and incapable of adjusting the many difficulties of bickering brigadiers. When he resigned in September, there was one all ready to fill his place; the wily Benjamin had thoroughly familiarized himself with the duties of the head of the all-important war department. President Davis offered him Walker's portfolio on September 17th, requesting him to retain his other post also until the middle of November.

The hitherto almost perennial smile faded away for a moment with the realization of the great importance attached to the new task. However, he was in robust health, capable of a vast amount of work, and deeply anxious to serve.

The Richmond correspondent of the New Orleans *Delta,* a paper which had become generally unfavorable to Benjamin, wrote home, September 28th, as follows: "The good effects of his presence in the War Department are already exhibited in his administration as compared with that of his predecessor. The duties of the War Department are, of course, excessively arduous and unremittent; but Mr. Benjamin manages to fulfill them all without exciting complaints of delay. He determines every question submitted to him with the promptness and the accuracy characteristic of his mind, while at the same time he exhibits administrative capacity of a high order and great organizing talents."

Under Benjamin's supervision, the War Department was thoroughly organized for efficient service. The immense mass of correspondence, which had formerly been allowed to accumulate till confusion and despair reigned, was disposed of on the day of its receipt, if that were humanly possible. Every one was assigned specific duties, and the Secretary saw to it that these duties were performed. By simple means he managed to save himself drudgery over details and to leave more time for the multifarious larger problems that must quite properly engage the attention of a Minister. At no time during his life had the new Secretary of War worked so hard—and at no previous time had his genius for organization shown itself to better advantage.

The nature of the matters toward which Benjamin

was required to show attention was the most varied imaginable. One of his first duties was the conduct of certain negotiations between the central government and the Virginia State Convention. His correspondence in this instance reveals the clear cut, precise and logical manner in which he proposed to carry on the business of his department:

> "Confederate States of America,
> "War Dept., Richmond, Nov. 22, 1861.

"Sir:

"Will not your convention do something to protect your own people against atrocious crimes, committed on their persons and property?

"There are, in the army, unfortunately, some desperate characters, men gathered from the outskirts and purlieus of large cities, who take advantage of the absence of the civil authorities to commit crimes, even murder, rape, and highway robbery, on the peaceful citizens in the neighborhood of the armies.

"For these offenses the punishment must be inflicted by the civil authorities. Our people must not lose their respect for law in the midst of this clash of arms. Some legislation is absolutely indispensable to provide for changing the venire; for carrying the accused into some county, where the process of law is not prevented by the presence of armies. There are murderers now in insecure custody at Manassas, who cannot be tried for want of a court there, and who will escape the just penalty of their crimes.

"The crimes committed by these men are not military offenses. If a soldier, rambling through the country, murders a farmer, or violates the honor of his wife or daughter, court martial cannot properly take cognizance of the offense, nor is it allowable to establish military commissions or tribunals in our country.

"I appeal to Virginian legislators for protection to Virginians, and this appeal will, I know, be responded to by prompt and efficient action.

"I am, very respectfully,
    "Your Obedient Servant,
        (Signed)   "J. P. BENJAMIN, *Sec. of War.*"
"To JOHN LETCHER,
    "Governor of Virginia"

The above letter shows Benjamin negotiating with the state government of Virginia. A few weeks later demand was exercised upon his tact and diplomacy in dealing with a military situation—somewhat petty in itself but important as being typical of considerable similar bickerings:

"Confederate States of America,
"War Department,
"Richmond, 27th Dec., 1861.

"Sir:

"The Adjutant General has, in accordance with the request of General William H. Whiting, placed his letter of 19th instant before the President, and I am instructed by him to reply as follows,

"The President has read with grave displeasure the very insubordinate letter of General Whiting in which he indulges in presumptuous censure of the orders of the Commander-in-chief, and tenders unasked advice to his superiors in command.

"The President does not desire to force on Brig. Gen. Whiting the command of the Brigade which had been assigned to him, and which it was supposed he would find himself honored in accepting, and you are requested to issue an order relieving Brig. Gen'l Whiting of the command of a brigade of five Mississippi regiments assigned to him by general orders Nos. 15 and 18, issued from this department.

"As there is no other brigade in the army of the Potomac not already provided with a commander under the general orders of the Department, the services of Brig. Gen'l Whiting will no longer be needed in command of troops.

"The President therefore further requests that Major W. H. Whiting of the Engineer Corps of the Confederate States be directed by your order to report for duty as an Engineer to Major General Jackson of the Valley District, where the services of this able engineer will be very useful to the army.

"In conclusion the President requests me to say that he trusts you will hereafter decline to forward to him communications of your subordinates having so obvious a tendency to excite a mutinous and disorganizing spirit in the army.

"I am, very respectfully,
"Yr. Obedient Servant,
(Signed) "J. P. BENJAMIN,
"Sec. of War."

"GENERAL JOSEPH E. JOHNSTON,
"Commander, Dept. of Northern Va."

Nor was this the only type of petty bickering that Benjamin was forced to interest himself in. Simultaneously, he was called upon to straighten out a nasty tangle involving the central government and the state of Virginia. An exchange of various letters took place between Charles Dirmmock, Colonel of Ordnance of Virginia, and J. P. Benjamin, Secretary of War for the

Confederacy—with Governor Letcher acting as intermediary and numerous Confederate army officers contributing notes of information to Benjamin's letters. The entire matter is a splendid illustration of the constant trouble between the central authority and the state government—due to the loosely arranged structure of the Confederacy.

Colonel Dirmmock was angry because the Virginia manufactured muskets were being altered at the Confederate armory and then were being reissued to Confederate troops from all over—without being properly credited to the account of the state of Virginia. Judah P. Benjamin took up the matter, calmly and carefully answering all questions—ever striving with unruffled dignity to keep things running smoothly. Finally, he wrote:

"Confederate States of America,
"War Dept., Richmond, Nov. 8, 1861.
"His Excellency JOHN LETCHER,
"Gov. of Virginia.
"SIR:
"I have referred to the chief of ordnance the letter of Col. Dirmmock of Nov. 2, which was enclosed by

your excellency to this dept., with your endorsement of Nov. 4th.

"In reply, I will quote from the report of Lieut. Col. Gorgas, which has just been submitted in reply to my enquiry upon the subject.

"Lieut. Col. Gorgas says:

" 'That the flint lock muskets in the hands of this dept. are received chiefly in exchange for better arms issued to troops. Very few have been collected. No scrutiny has been made as to whether they were of Virginia manufacture or otherwise; and they are altered and placed in the hands of troops without question as to whether the troops are Virginians, or from other states of the Confederacy.

" 'The State of Virginia would of course be the gainer in the transaction, since Virginian arms, altered at the expense of the Confederacy, will revert to her at the close of the war, without charge of alteration as no account is kept against her on this score.

" 'Presuming that the workshops employed by the state are fully occupied, as should be the case, there could be no increment of credit to the state ordnance dept., were the ordnance dept. of the Confederate States to desist from altering the state arms, assuming such to be a fact.'

"Will your excellency be good enough to communicate this answer, which I hope will be satisfactory to Col. Dirmmock.

"Very respectfully,
"Your obedient Servant,
(Signed) "J. P. BENJAMIN,
"*Secretary of War.*

"P.S. In compliance with your excellency's request I enclose herewith the letter of Col. Dirmmock, of which I have retained a copy to be placed on file in this dept."

· · · · · ·

Through the early winter of 1862 Benjamin continued to discharge, easily and efficiently, the varied collection of tasks that presented themselves. However, fortune began to turn its back on several Confederate military operations; and the position of Secretary of War became far from an enviable post. On February 16th, the plans of Albert Sidney Johnston for invading Kentucky and Tennessee received a severe shock. Fort Donelson surrendered unconditionally to General U. S. Grant, with 12,000 men and 40 pieces of artillery. The blame for this could hardly be placed upon the government—but it was a very appropriate corollary of the Roanoke Island disaster, which caused Judah P. Benjamin no end of discomfort and annoyance.

"THE BRAINS OF THE CONFEDERACY"

The Confederates, having failed in the effort to keep the Federal forces outside of Hatteras, had hastily fortified Roanoke Island, commanding the passage from Pamlico to Albemarle Sound, and thus protecting not only a number of small yet useful ports, but also the approach to Norfolk from the rear. General Benjamin Huger, with about 15,000 men, was in command of the department at Norfolk. To General Henry A. Wise was entrusted the task of completing the poor fortifications on the island and defending it. In spite of urgent appeals for ammunition, General Wise got no help from the war office or from General Huger. On February 8th, the small force on the island was overwhelmed, and most of it captured. The loss of this strategic point, however, was far more severe than would appear from the casualty list. In its consequences it was, perhaps, more irreparable than the surrender of Donelson; the gradual loss of seaports was making it difficult for the Confederacy to breathe.

It was clear that General Wise was not at fault; some other victim had to be found on whom to lay the blame for Roanoke Island. Wise was something of a popular idol; and when he charged that the Secretary of War had paid no attention to his requisitions for materials and ammunition, the fury of the press and the politicians was turned loose upon Mr. Benjamin. The Richmond *Examiner* declared:

"So curious is the ignorance and complacency of our government in this matter, that we are advised that, though the defense of Roanoke Island was urged upon the Secretary of War for weeks before the demonstration of the enemy was made, Mr. Benjamin insisted strenuously and to the last moment that Roanoke Island was positively not the object of the enemy's attack, but that a great battle was to come off at Pensacola, for which he was busy in preparation, sending to the Gulf coast all the shot, shell, and ammunition that could be gathered.... With equal disregard and the same stupid complacency was treated the protest of General Wise, made at the time of his taking command of Roanoke Island. These are strange facts; but they are true. It is possible that the persistent delusion of Mr. Benjamin as to the designs of the enemy on the coast may be accounted for on the supposition that his mind was abused by the duplicity of the spies he employs. It is notorious that the easy credulity of the Secretary has more than once been imposed upon by double-dealing spies and covert agents of the Lincoln government.... We are surprised by each movement of the enemy; the War Department seems to know no more of his plans and intentions than the children in the streets of Richmond; the credulity of its Secretary is absolutely astonishing."

In the face of such popular distrust, Mr. Benjamin's usefulness as Secretary of War was obviously ended. The Congress called a special committee to investigate the disaster and to allocate the blame. Until 1887, the outside world knew nothing further of the matter than the fact that the committee report found Benjamin to be guilty. On March 27th, it became known that the Secretary of War had been dismissed, or had resigned. His enemies were overjoyed.

But the following day it was announced that Benjamin had been appointed Secretary of State. Even before the Congressional Committee could officially publish its report against the late Secretary of War, Benjamin had been transferred to that position, for which more than any other he was preëminently qualified.

In 1887 Colonel Charles Marshall, who had been military secretary to Robert E. Lee, delivered a momentous lecture at Richmond. His topic was "Secret History of the Confederacy" and one of his most important revelations was in regard to the Roanoke Island disaster. He told how "Early in 1862, Gen. Wise, in command at Roanoke Island, made a requisition for powder. It was not sent. A second and a third call were likewise ignored—and on February 8, Roanoke Island fell. Wise complained, and in compliance with his request a committee of Congress investigated his failure to send powder. When the investigating body met, Benjamin in a very few words told them why it was not sent—*there was none to send,* a temporary shortage of munitions existing! The committee, being about to rise, Benjamin asked if it would not have a very harmful effect on the people if the true state of affairs was disclosed. The committee thought it would. The Cabinet official then suggested that the report of the committee censure him for not sending the powder. This was done, and, to keep up appearances, Benjamin sent in his resignation as Secretary of War. Except to Davis and a few other high officials the truth of the matter remained secret. It was his resignation under a cloud that probably caused such dislike in some quarters to Benjamin—a dislike that was only heightened by the promptness with which he was appointed to a higher portfolio."

Col. Marshall related that he had these facts in a letter from Benjamin, written to him at the time they occurred. That Davis appointed Benjamin Secretary of State the day following his resignation of the War portfolio appears to be splendid circumstantial evidence in support of Marshall's version.

To the Confederate government at large Benjamin had proven his tremendous executive abilities in organizing the War Department. To Jefferson Davis at least he had demonstrated, in his conduct during the Roanoke Island investigation, a unique philosophy—the philosophy of genuine, unselfish patriotism.

At the end of March, 1862—calmly ignoring the general disapproval at his promotion while "under a cloud," Judah P. Benjamin ascended the bridge of the Confederate ship of state. Unperturbed, he took a firm grasp on the helm of the "Lost Cause."

CHAPTER VII

"THE PREMIER OF THE LOST CAUSE"

THE new Secretary of State was well suited for his position. From the very inception of the Confederate government he had loomed up as the most potent and influential of the President's advisers. Now, in addition to those duties, falling directly within his department's jurisdiction, he continued to assist with all the other important questions which arose. It became proverbial among those connected with the administration that to almost every weighty inquiry, explanation or petition, the President would reply: "Take that matter up with Mr. Benjamin."

The chief minister was always ready for work. Sometimes, with half an hour's recess, he would remain with the President from ten in the morning until nine at night, and together they would traverse all the difficulties that encompassed the beleaguered South. According to Mrs. Jefferson Davis, "Both worked like galley-slaves, early and late. Mr. Davis came home a mass of throbbing nerves, perfectly exhausted; but Mr. Benjamin was always fresh and buoyant. There was one striking peculiarity about his temperament. No matter what befell our armies, after he had done all in his power to prevent or rectify it, he was never depressed."

Benjamin entered very little into the social life of the city. Even had he wished to, he had no time for it. His favorite recreation—in those few moments of leisure he was able to enjoy—was backgammon and similar games of chance; he was an inveterate gambler. In addition he would always find a little time to spend with his beloved poets—Horace and Tennyson. Perhaps he drew from them some of the inspiration which enabled him to keep up so terrific a pace in such a remarkable manner. He was often pointed out as he hurried to work in the morning—"There goes Mr. Benjamin, smiling as usual."

Immediately following his appointment to the

Department of State, the new chief minister communicated with his agent in London:

"From J. P. Benjamin, Secretary of State, Confederate States, to J. M. Mason, Commissioner of the Confederate States to Great Britain.

"Department of State,
"Richmond, April 5, 1862.

"SIR: The inauguration of the permanent Government of the Confederate States having taken place in accordance with the Constitution and the Laws on the 22nd February last, the President determined to make certain changes in his Cabinet, and the Department of State was confided to my charge. The Cabinet was formed on the 19th ulto., and is constituted as follows, viz.:

J. P. Benjamin, of Louisiana . . . . Secretary of State
C. G. Memminger, of South Carolina,
                              Secretary of Treasury
Thos. H. Watts, of Alabama . . . . . Attorney-General
Geo. W. Randolph, of Virginia . . . Secretary of War
S. R. Mallory, of Florida . . . . . . Secretary of Navy
J. H. Reagan, of Texas . . . . Postmaster-General

"All of these gentlemen have entered on the discharge of their duties, except Hon. Thos. H. Watts, who has not yet arrived in Richmond.

"THE PREMIER OF THE LOST CAUSE"

"In assuming the charge of this Department under the permanent Government, it is deemed expedient to keep the archives separate from those of the Provisional Government. Hence a new series of numbers will be commenced in the dispatches, and this is numbered 'one.'"

With the sending of the above quoted notice began Benjamin's three years of diplomatic maneuvering. In considering his services to the Confederacy, his conduct of its foreign relations is of the highest importance. The financial administration of the Government was largely dependent upon European recognition and intervention, not merely because credit for borrowing purposes was upon this achievement, but because necessary loans could be negotiated satisfactorily only abroad. So also, the problems of creating a navy and instigating European disregard for the alleged blockade of Confederate ports, were almost wholly dependent upon diplomatic successes.

The two principal countries here involved were England and France, and at an early stage, it became manifest that European diplomatic connections required them to agree upon concerted action. As regards

England, Benjamin's policy was based almost entirely on his acceptance of the theory that "Cotton is King." He believed that the cotton famine which was resulting from the War and which he utilized thruout as the basis for negotiations with Europe, would drive England into a recognition of the Confederacy and intervention. An investigation into the conduct of British relations with the Confederacy tends to confirm the view that he nearly succeeded, that actual starvation was narrowly avoided for a large section of the English people in consequence of the War. John Stuart Mill has described the rush of nearly the whole upper and middle classes, even those who passed for Liberals, into a furious pro-Southern partisanship. The London *Times* and the *Saturday Review,* for the press, were outspoken on the side of Southern independence. They asked why should England be compelled to suffer a cotton famine and little less than industrial ruin, in order that the inevitable success of the Davis government might be for a short time postponed?

But the highly desirable goal of British recognition was never reached. The intention of Russell and Palmerston to avoid complications with the United States—the unmistakable hostility of Russell toward the South, after the *Trent* affair—the ingenious diplomacy of Charles Francis Adams—and the pro-Northern sympathy of the English laboring classes—all united to argue against recognition.

True it is that on Oct. 7, 1862, Gladstone declared—"There is no doubt that Jefferson Davis and other leaders of the South have made an army; they are making, it appears, a navy; and they have made what is more than either—they have made a nation." The effects of this assertion, however, were offset by the great public meetings held on New Year's Eve in London, Manchester, and Sheffield—to show the appreciation of the English laboring classes for Lincoln's stand on the Emancipation Proclamation. Even the most supercilious of the Parliament, still largely hostile to the North, could not afford to ignore the voice of the multitude.

Then came Chancellorsville and the last opportunity for the pro-Southern English group to argue recognition of the South. This was done by Roebuck—who went so far as to try to destroy the Russell Cabinet.

But the Government rallied to the latter's support—and when, a few days later, the news of Gettysburg and Vicksburg arrived, the anti-Federal ideas of Gladstone and Roebuck were completely discredited.

Following this came the incident of the iron clad rams—when Charles Francis Adams remarked, "Your Lordship, this means war"—and, with its conclusion in the fall of 1863, the last real danger of English recognition of the Confederacy passed away.

Confederate diplomacy, however, won many victories short of actual recognition in England, strengthening the credit and standing of the Davis government. The decision of the Alabama Claims in favor of the United States indicates that Great Britain had been induced by Confederate efforts to favor unduly the designs of the South, in the matter of naval affairs. Benjamin's arguments, based upon the high tariff walls erected by the North, in favor of European recognition and intervention, were ingenious.

The nature of Benjamin's futile efforts to secure English recognition is clearly revealed in a lengthy memorandum of a conversation between Mason and Lord Palmerston, which took place at Cambridge

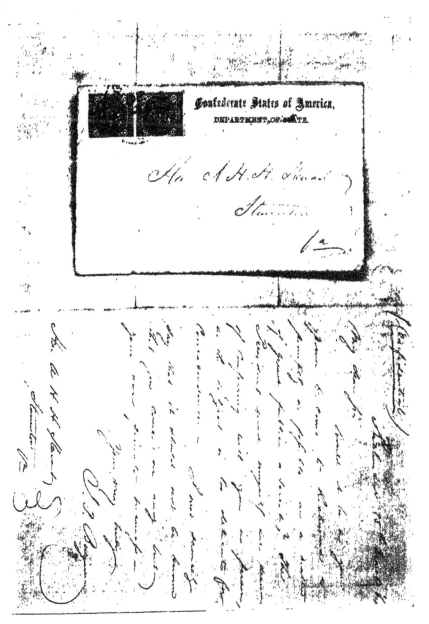

AN ILLUSTRATION OF BENJAMIN'S OFFICIAL CORRESPONDENCE

This letter, in the possession of the Confederate White House at Richmond, is one of very few in existence. The Secretary burned nearly all of his correspondence before leaving the capital.

House on March 14, 1865. This meeting took place at Benjamin's request and the resulting interchange of ideas was sent on to him at Richmond. Mason presented his case: "Confederate States feel that some unknown obstacle is preventing England's recognition ... very disappointed ... what is the obstacle? ... South is annoyed at Her Majesty's Government withholding recognition ... resents implication that South is simply in rebellion."

Lord Palmerston was obviously toying with the Confederate Commissioner, as is evidenced by the concluding section of the memorandum. "He [Lord P.] said that although there had been no formal recognition of the South in all the attributes of a political power, its having been acknowledged as a belligerent was a disclaimer of anything like a rebellion. His Lordship's manner throughout the interview was uniformly conciliatory and kind. He begged me to be assured that he would always be glad to see me whenever I had anything which I desired to communicate to him."

As regards France, Benjamin's efforts seem to have been more comprehensive. He was well acquainted with the temper of the French nation and its monarch,

Napoleon III, having made annual trips to France during many years preceding the war, on one of which he had had a personal interview with the Emperor in regard to Southern problems. Mercier, the French Ambassador to the United States, who had been a close friend of Benjamin's prior to the war, was induced to pay a visit to Richmond in the spring of 1862, and was very friendly towards the interests of the Confederacy. Particular efforts were made to secure French aid in the direction of recognition and intervention, but, however probable the success of these efforts appeared to be at different times, the agreement with England for concerted action and general European politics prevented the success of these endeavors.

But, just as in the case of England, even though actual recognition was not obtained, nonetheless Benjamin did achieve certain triumphs during his diplomatic relations with France. His close personal ties with the Erlanger family of Paris proved invaluable in the negotiation of the Erlanger loans, by which the Confederacy secured its most important financial assistance abroad. A somewhat amusing incident occurred in connection with this particular loan—significant for its showing the general unpopularity of the administration and the distrust felt in many quarters for Benjamin's power.

Gov. Foote, in attacking the administration à propos of a visit of two hours' duration paid by M. Erlanger at the State Department, during which the conversation was conducted in French, said in a speech to the Confederate House of Representatives: "On the occasion of the recent visit of Mr. Erlanger, Minister Plenipotentiary and Envoy Extraordinary from his Highness, the Emperor of France, to his Highness, the would-be Emperor of the Confederate States, Judas Iscariot Benjamin spoke French for two hours," referring, with biting sarcasm, to Cicero's having spoken Greek for two hours when Julius Cæsar was thrice tendered the crown.

Before leaving the subject of Benjamin's relations with France, mention should be made of the ingenious methods he suggested to his agent, Slidell, for influencing the Emperor's government. These methods included carefully exerted pressure upon the Chambers of Commerce in the principal French cities so that these organizations would petition the Emperor to intervene to any extent necessary to restore commercial relations with the Southern States. Slidell's efforts never achieved signal success—tho the ingenuity of the methods employed must nonetheless evoke admiration.

Closely connected with his diplomacy in France was Benjamin's conduct of the relations between the Confederate States and Mexico. During the summer of 1863, he had made overtures to the Mexican Imperialists. In December, 1863, a confidential agent of Almonte, now head of the Imperial Government in Mexico, called upon Quintero, the Davis agent, in Monterey, and informed him that the Regent had already suggested to Napoleon the advisability of recognizing the Confederacy, and was now anxiously awaiting the arrival of a commission from the South. The communication of these facts led Judah P. Benjamin to send William Preston as Envoy Extraordinary and Minister Plenipotentiary to Mexico. He was instructed (Jan., 1864) to ascertain whether he would at once be received as the accredited ambassador of an independent government. Upon the arrival of Maximilian he was to propose a treaty of alliance of ten years' duration for mutual defence against the United States. A treaty of amity and commerce was to be effected, also, and likewise a free passage across Sonora and Chihuahua to the Pacific. When the new Emperor arrived, however, he gave no intention of a desire for official relations with the Confederacy, and Preston was at length recalled.

Maximilian was no doubt influenced in this course of action by Louis Napoleon. The minister of the Juárez government at Washington and the Minister of the United States in France had kept Seward well informed, and his constant watch over, and protest against, Napoleon's actions had led the French ruler to assume an attitude of cautious duplicity, very exasperating to the Confederate Secretary of State. In fact, Benjamin virtually despaired of aid from this quarter after September, 1864, when he wrote to Mason at Paris—"The Emperor of the French professed an earnest sympathy for us and a desire to serve us, which, however sincere at the time, have yielded to the first suggestion of advantages to be gained by rendering assistance to our enemies."

One of Benjamin's most unique undertakings was his effort to offset the work of the Federal recruiting agents in Europe. Ireland in particular had proven an almost limitless source of supply for the filling of the Union ranks. Every inducement was offered by the Lincoln government to make immigration more attractive. High pay, easily obtained citizenship, grants of land in the West, were all held out as the potential rewards of those who should come to the United States. Superior man power was the weapon upon which the Federal government had come to rely most heavily; and no stone was left unturned in the effort to strengthen its position in this respect.

The Secretary of State determined to do all in his power to defeat the activities of the Northern recruiting officers abroad, and began the task of setting up an organization of his own in Ireland. His plan of attack is revealed in his comprehensive dispatch to Lieutenant J. L. Capston:—

"Department of State,
"Richmond, 3rd July, 1863.

"Sir:

"You have in accordance with your proposal made to

this department been detailed by the Secretary of War for Special Service under my orders.

"The duty which it is proposed to entrust to you is that of a private and confidential agent of this government, for the purpose of proceeding to Ireland and there using all legitimate means to enlighten the population as to the true nature and character of the contest now waged on this continent, with the view of defeating the agents of the United States to obtain in Ireland recruits for their armies. It is understood that under the guise of assisting needy persons to emigrate a regular organization has been formed in Ireland of agents who leave untried no methods of deceiving the laboring population into emigrating for the ostensible purpose of seeking employment in the United States—but really for recruiting in the Federal Armies.

"The means to be employed by you can scarcely be suggested from this side, but they are to be confined to such as are strictly legitimate, honorable, and proper. We rely on truth and justice alone. Throw yourself as much as possible into close communication with the people, where the agents of our enemies are at work. Inform them by every means you can devise of the true purposes of those who seek to induce them to emigrate. Explain to them the nature of the warfare which is carried on here. Picture to them the fate of their unhappy countrymen who have already fallen victims to the arts of the Federals. Relate to them the story of Meagher's Brigade, its formation, and its fate. Explain to them that they will be called on to meet Irishmen in battle, and thus to imbue their hands in the blood of their own friends and perhaps kinsmen, in a quarrel which does not concern them and in which all the feelings of a common humanity should induce them to refuse taking part against us. Contrast the policy of the Federal and the Confederate States in former times in their treatment of foreigners, in order to satisfy Irishmen where true sympathy in their favor was found.

"At the North, the Know Nothing Party, based on hatred to foreigners and especially to Catholics, was triumphant in its career. In the South it was crushed, Virginia taking the lead in trampling it under foot. In this War such has been the hatred of the New England Puritans to Irishmen and Catholics, that in several instances the Chapels and places of Worship of the Irish Catholics have been burned or shamefully desecrated by the Regiments of Volunteers from New England. These facts have been published in northern papers. Take the New York *Freeman's Journal* and you will see shocking details not coming from Confederate Sources, but from the Officers of the United States themselves. Lay all these matters fully before the people who are now called upon to join these ferocious persecutors in the destruction of this nation where all religions and all nationalities meet equal justice and protection, both from the people and from the laws.

"These views may be urged by any proper means you can devise through the press; by mixing with the people themselves; and by disseminating the facts amongst persons who have influence with the people.

"The laws of England must be strictly respected and obeyed by you. While prudence dictates that you should not reveal your agency nor the purposes for which you go abroad, it is not desired nor expected that you use any dishonest disguise or false pretenses. Your mission is, although secret, honorable, and the means employed must be such as this government may fearlessly avow and openly justify, if your conduct should ever be called into question. On this point there must be no room whatever for doubt or cavil.

"The government expects much from your zeal, activity, and discretion. You will be furnished with letters of introduction to our agents abroad. You will receive the same pay as you get as 1st Lieut. of Cavalry, namely twenty-one pounds per month, being about equal to one hundred dollars. Your passage to and from Europe will be provided by this department. If you need any small sums for disbursement of expenses connected with your duties, such as cost of printing and the like, you will apply to the agent to whom I give you a letter and who will provide the funds, if he approves the expenditure.

"You will report your proceedings to this department through the agent to whom your letter of introduction is addressed, as often at least as once a month.

"I am, Sir, respectfully,
"Your Obedient Servant,
"J. P. BENJAMIN,
"Sec'y of State.

"LIEUT. J. L. CAPSTON."

The sending of this letter was contemporaneous with, and probably tied carefully to, Benjamin's efforts for securing Papal intervention on behalf of the Confederacy. The victories at Gettysburg and Vicksburg were more than sufficient, however, to make these efforts futile. The possibilities of diplomatic success were growing less with each succeeding northern triumph.

. . . .

The fastidious Benjamin retained his bright, cheerful aspect thru the dark days which began now to descend upon Richmond. The effects of the Federal Blockade were felt even in the highest official circles. Mrs. Davis would occasionally invite the Secretary of State to tea with such words as "Do come this afternoon; we succeeded in running the blockade last week." All of which meant "real coffee," good tea, preserved fruits and sometimes even anchovy toast. Such luxury was very welcome to the epicurean tastes of the chief minister.

During the year 1864 Lincoln had found the man for whom he had been searching. And the gentleman in question had decided to "fight it out on this line if it takes all summer." Simultaneously General Sherman was cutting the South in two by his march thru the heart of Georgia. The ranks of Lee's army were growing less formidable in appearance with each succeeding battle. Where one northern regiment was wiped out, two sprang into its place; but the Confederacy had no such unlimited supply of man-power, and its shrinking forces continued to melt away.

Mr. Benjamin, realizing that matters had reached a desperate point, determined to call forth desperate remedies. He sought to convince his chief that it was time for the South to make one last bid for victory. First, the ranks of the army must be refilled by following Lincoln's example of enlisting the negro. Secondly, European intervention, which should raise the blockade, must be obtained; since other methods had not succeeded, the Confederacy must try to influence England by promising emancipation of the slaves.

The President was extremely reluctant, at first, to follow his minister's proposal in regard to the recruiting of negro soldiers. However, when General Lee added his approval to the plan, Davis gave his support. His recommendation that Congress give him the power to fill the ranks of the army in this fashion gave rise to bitter wrangling. Although the force of Lee's influence was the deciding factor in putting the measure thru, the press denounced Benjamin for all its odious features. The unpopularity, which his promotion "under a cloud" had brought forth before, was again rampant, and demands were made for his resignation. He was also attacked on the score of his religion in the bitterest and most fanatical manner. In this difficult time, as always, Jefferson Davis stood

CONFEDERATE CHIEFTAINS

by him—unmoved by the cries of the mob, loyal to the one whose deep patriotism he recognized and whose true worth he well appreciated. Unruffled, the Secretary of State went about his business, his enigmatic smile still in evidence.

The plan for enlisting negroes fell far short of success. Mass meetings were held and enthusiastic speeches were made, but these failed to furnish the badly needed recruits. "The Jubilee was comin'" and "Marse Lincum's boys were winnin' too many victories" by the time the plan was invoked.

In the meanwhile, Benjamin's other desperate plan was being worked out in Europe. Feeling that Mason and Slidell might not be thoroughly in accord with the new plan, he dispatched his friend, Congressman Kenner of Louisiana, to offer emancipation in exchange for recognition. Armed with full instructions and entrusted with great powers, the new envoy slipped through the Union lines into New York and thence made his way to Europe. Once there, he ignored his instructions and commenced to do his work through Mason and Slidell. The latter arranged an interview for him with the French Minister of Foreign Affairs, an interview which netted nothing but a promise to think the matter over. Having met with so little success in Paris, Kenner hastened across the Channel on March 3rd to do the business of the Confederacy in England. He immediately entered into negotiations with London bankers for the sale of cotton, should recognition be obtained. While he was thus occupied, Mason arranged to bring the new proposal from Benjamin before Lord Palmerston. This was accomplished on March 31st, the British Minister listening with intent to the offer that the Confederacy would abolish slavery, if that were the obstacle to recognition. At the end of the interview, he assured Mason that his government's objections were not based on the slavery question but on the broad matters of policy so often discussed by the two in the months previous. The offer had been made in vain. Whether it would have met greater success if proposed earlier is a debatable question. It had obviously come too late for any possible accomplishment; a few days after Mason's conversation with Palmerston, Richmond fell into the hands of the Federal troops.

· · · · · · · ·

President Davis was attending the Sunday morning services in St. Paul's church when the news of Lee's retreat was brought to him. An officer tiptoed down the aisle, whispered in his ear, and the two hurried out together. The next few hours were busy ones for the chief executive and his official family. For some weeks, however, the packing up of government papers had been quietly going on—and most things were in readiness for immediate removal. The Confederate leaders hastened to Danville, where they established temporary headquarters. Among those who accompanied them was the Reverend Dr. Hoge, patriotic pastor of St. Paul's and warm friend of Judah P. Benjamin.

The Presbyterian minister was well known in Danville and was invited to put up at the home of a banker friend, Mr. J. M. Johnston. He insisted that Benjamin share his room, a proposal in which the banker's family enthusiastically concurred. During the week they remained there, the fugitive Secretary of State endeared himself to his companions by his continued cheerfulness.

On April 9th word was received that Lee had surrendered. Davis and his companions prepared to retreat further south. The first stage of the trip was by rail and brought the runaway government to Greensboro, North Carolina. After a few days here, the journey was renewed, this time by army wagons and on horseback. Benjamin, being short, stout and unaccustomed to riding, travelled with several others in an ambulance drawn by a pair of broken-down old grays. When they rode along at night, the wagon's sole illumination was the bright glow of the chief minister's cheerful cigar. The others proceeded in glum silence, while Benjamin's silvery voice rose now and again to recite Tennyson's poetry for their comfort.

The party proceeded to Charlotte and Abbeville, thence on to Washington, Georgia. Here news reached them of General Johnston's surrender. Benjamin realized that the last hopes of the Confederacy were gone, and that his duty was now to his almost forgotten family in Paris. His face was filled with sadness as he approached his chief and asked, "As I can serve our people no more just now, will you consent to my making an effort to escape thru Florida? If you should

"THE PREMIER OF THE LOST CAUSE"

ever be in a condition to require me again, I shall answer your call at once."

And so we come to the final word in the American career of Judah P. Benjamin, a career that placed him in the front rank of those gallant gentlemen who followed "The Lost Cause." Reflecting for a moment on his brilliant achievements under the Stars and Bars, and taking the liberty of a momentary glance into the remarkable comeback he would make after all seemed lost, we are tempted to quote the words of his favorite poet:

> "Tho much is taken, much abides; and tho
> We are not now that strength which in old days
> Moved earth and heaven; that which we are, we are."

CHAPTER VIII

TRANSPLANTED GENIUS AND RECOVERED FORTUNE

THE fugitive Secretary was a sad and weary figure as he made his way toward Florida. A victorious, passionate North was clamoring for the capture of the "Rebel Leaders," and it was necessary for Benjamin to travel in disguise. Dressed in rough homespun clothes, which were given him by the kind wife of a farmer, he journeyed along the back roads. When he was accosted by people, he assumed a false name and professed to be looking for a site in Florida where he might settle. Forced to travel on horseback, he was unable to cover more than thirty miles a day, and it was weeks before he reached his destination on the coast of Florida. There he learned that a reward had been placed on the head of Jefferson Davis, and that the fate of any Confederate leader falling into Northern hands might be a hard one. He determined to risk every peril in an effort to reach England.

It required almost a month to complete arrangements for his departure from the Florida coast. He finally secured two trusty persons to accompany him in the dangerous attempt to cross the Gulf of Mexico with a small boat. The yawl in question contained no sleeping accommodations or covered quarters whatever. Through frequent squalls and choppy seas, it sailed along, bringing its passengers at last to the Bemini Isles. Seventeen days and six hundred miles, a rather severe trip for a man well over fifty! Benjamin breathed a sigh of relief as he noted the Union Jack floating over the customs-house; all danger of capture was gone; after living most of his life as an American, he was once more under the British flag.

But the perils which were to beset him, until at last he should arrive in London, were not yet ended. Three days after he had reached Bemini, he embarked on a small sloop, bound for the larger island of Nassau. At half-past seven the next morning, the sloop foundered and commenced to sink rapidly. The small crew and the single passenger had barely enough time to jump into a lifeboat when the vessel went down. There was but one oar in the tiny skiff and the efforts to reach land were necessarily feeble.

Fortunately, an English brig sighted the victims in the early afternoon. By five o'clock the former Secretary was being warmly greeted by Captain Stuart of her Majesty's Light-House Yacht *Georgia*. The vessel was on a tour of the Bahama lighthouses, but its commander turned from his scheduled path to land Benjamin back at Bemini, which he reached for the second time on July 15th. He then chartered another sloop and after a stormy trip finally reached Nassau. A steamer was leaving the following day for Cuba, and, as there was no occasion for delay, he took passage on it.

In Havana, the fugitive rested for a couple of weeks. Providing himself with comfortable clothing again, he proceeded to enjoy what entertainment the city afforded. General Kirby Smith, who had escaped thru Mexico, arrived in Cuba at about the same time and the two spent hours together in an anxious interchange of news. They were both especially concerned with the fate of Jefferson Davis, who had been thrown into prison by the Northern authorities. Benjamin, who loved his former chief to the very depth of his nature, declared: "No nobler gentleman, no purer man, no more exalted patriot ever drew breath; and eternal infamy will blacken the base and savage wretches who are now taking advantage of their brief grasp of power to wreak a cowardly vengeance on his honored head."

He celebrated the fifty-fourth anniversary of his birth by boarding the small steamer which was to take him to the island of St. Thomas. Here, he spent a week revisiting the scenes of his childhood, while he awaited the arrival of the large vessel which was to take him to England. On August 13th the ocean-going ship departed, but when only ninety miles out at sea was found to be on fire in the forehold. Through dint of great exertion and discipline the fire was kept under control and practically extinguished by the time the boat had staggered back to port. Three days were required to remove the burned cargo and repair the damaged sections. At last, the ship's prow was once more set in the direction of England, and this time she completed her voyage without mishap.

Benjamin was compelled to remain a week in London before crossing the Channel to see his family. Once his business was completed, he hastened to Paris and joined them. What a reunion it was, this first meeting with the loved ones he had not seen during more than five long years. He was forced to look again and again at the dainty young woman who called him "Mon Père." Was this lovely Parisian indeed his little Ninette? His obligation as the head of his family commenced to weigh heavily upon him. Natalie must be maintained in the luxury to which she was accustomed; his daughter must have an ample dowry. He must begin to rebuild his shattered fortunes at once.

While in Paris he dined with his former agent, Slidell, and was introduced by him to a number of prominent bankers. One of these intimated to him that should he decide to live in France, an honorable and lucrative position would be opened to him in financial circles. His old friend from New Orleans, the prominent Madame de Pontalba, offered all sorts of assistance, were he to take up his residence at Paris.

However, the former Confederate premier had other plans in mind. A career at the British bar appealed to him as the most independent and promising future he could start upon.

After a comparatively short visit with his family, he recrossed the Channel and proceeded to London. The great kindness and distinction with which he was received by leading Englishmen of the day strengthened his intention to apply for admission to the bar. Lord Campbell and Sir James Ferguson called on him immediately to offer their assistance. Disraeli wrote from the country, where he was vacationing, that he wished to be of service. The fame of the Confederate chieftain had preceded him, and the friendly doors of London society were opened to him.

As had happened twice before in his colorful career the most pressing problem he had to face was a financial one. And just as on those two occasions he had tackled the difficulties before him with buoyant courage and cheerfulness, so now again did this fifty-five-year-old fighter buckle down to reality. He had staked his all on the Confederacy, and nearly all was lost. Of his once great fortune scarce twenty thousand dollars remained, the proceeds from the sale of some cotton which he had managed to land in England. Six months after his arrival in Europe the greater part of this was swept away, when the firm of Overend, Gurney and Company, with whom it had been invested, failed.

As soon as the opportunity was given, he looked into the requirements for admission to the bar, and on Jan. 12, 1866, entered as a student at Lincoln's Inn. At the same time, scornful of the many offers of pecuniary assistance that were made to him, he commenced to write articles for the daily papers. This work brought him about five pounds a week and thus supplied him with a means of subsistence; what funds he had been able to salvage from the Overend, Gurney failure were turned over to his family in Paris.

. . . .

The frequent visitor to the Inns of Court received something of a shock when he looked in on the Lincoln's dining hall during the Spring of 1866. The first casual glance revealed everything to be quite in order. The tables at the head of the room were reserved as always for the older leaders of the bar, and our visitor noted with satisfaction the familiar faces of Lord Brougham, Sir Roundell Palmer, and Sir Hugh Cairnes. The next set of tables accommodated in proper fashion the half-hundred or so barristers generally found there. But he did see a striking irregularity in the third section where more than a hundred and fifty students were taking their dinner at tables of four each. His very first glance distinguished one individual from all the rest. Over there, chatting with a trio, fresh from either Oxford or Cambridge, sat a short, stout gentleman, who must be well past fifty!

Relishing his "joint and greens" with all the gusto of a contented epicure, this strange-looking student paused only for an occasional terse remark to his companions. On each such occasion, they would stop their heated argument for a moment, regard their friend with grateful respect, and then proceed once more to discussing the technicalities of the law.

Our visitor edged nearer to the table he had been watching just as the waiter was setting down a huge dish of cheddar cheese. He was surprised to hear the older man shift the conversation from the required field of the law to a series of witty anecdotes. The last of these was in the dialect common to the American darkey and brought forth roars of delight from the youthful audience. "But now, gentlemen," the older man concluded, "I must be off to the antechamber and rid myself of this robe which you people regard as so essential to the enjoyment of a meal here. I must hurry over to Mr. Charles Pollock's chambers, where I am serving my office apprenticeship. Cheerio." He rose, nodded his head, and left.

The three youngsters called out "Cheerio" and "Good luck to you, Sir," as our puzzled visitor moved away.

In less than six months after he had entered Lincoln's, Benjamin was called to the bar. The authorities were wise enough to see the absurdity in requiring him to spend the usual three years of preliminary study. However, a conservative respect for established rules did for a time threaten to impede. The influence of several Lords Justices, who were Benchers of Lincoln's Inn, was brought to bear and the one-time leader of the Louisiana Bar was finally exempted from the customary routine. Instead of seventy-two dinners at the hall of the Society he was asked to attend but a half-dozen. At the same time he commenced to "read law" in the Chambers of Mr. Charles Pollock, son of the chief Baron of the Exchequer. On June 6, 1866, he was admitted.

A powerful factor in his being able to achieve his goal so quickly was the peculiar circumstances of his nationality. Born of British parents and under the British flag, he was able to dismiss his forty-odd years of American citizenship as tho they had never been. The old axiom, "Once a Briton, always a Briton," was invoked in his favor, and from the very first he was received by his London colleagues as one of themselves.

No sooner had he been called to the bar, than he began to look about for suitable offices. After some little delay he secured what he wanted at number 4 Lamb Buildings, The Temple. His chambers there were his permament headquarters during the remainder of his active life.

The new barrister had not long to wait for clients. In addition to the excellent reputation which his American achievements had given him, Benjamin possessed certain distinct advantages over his brother advocates. And these were quickly recognized. His original legal training had been within the State of Louisiana where the law administered was that which had been the law of France before the formulation of the Code Napoleon. This system, derived originally from the great Roman code of Justinian, was also the basis of practice thruout the rest of Continental Europe and differed decidedly from the principles of "Stare Decisis" used by the English. Benjamin was thoroughly familiar with both and as a result was in a peculiarly advantageous position whenever cases requiring such familiarity arose. Appeals were constantly being brought to the Privy Council from British colonies that were formerly French, and on such occasions the ex-premier of the Confederacy towered above his fellows.

Another distinct advantage enjoyed by the newcomer lay in the fact that an American advocate was trained both as a solicitor and a barrister. In England, on the contrary, one became either an adviser, chained to a desk, or a strictly trial lawyer. While Benjamin entered upon the duties of the latter, he was nonetheless thoroughly acquainted with the work of the man in the office.

From the very beginning he worked with the same tireless energy that had characterized his early years at the Louisiana Bar. His old love for his profession renewed its hold stronger with each succeeding week. A few months after his entrance to practice, he wrote to the former Confederate Commissioner, Mason:

"I have as you know been called to the bar, and have chosen the Northern Circuit, which embraces Liverpool. I have attended assizes at Liverpool, and have as yet no reason to complain. Michaelmas term commences on the 29th instant, and I may have a chance to appear in some cases. My time is spent in close study, and I have not played in a game of whist since your departure. I am as much interested in my profession as when I first commenced as a boy, and am rapidly recovering all that I had partially forgotten in the turmoil of public affairs."

. . . .

It is early in the year 1867. The scene is a dignified English Court of Chancery, Vice Chancellor James sitting. The case on trial is the "United States vs. McRae, Ex-Agent for the Confederate States of America." The plaintiff is suing to compel McRae to render an account of all funds and property which had come into his hands as Agent for the Confederacy.

Counsel for the Plaintiff has closed. Mr. Kay, Leader

for the defendant, finishes his argument. It is becoming apparent that the Vice Chancellor is about to send the case for an accounting and reserve it for further consideration. Such a decision would obviously be fatal to the defendant.

At this point, the Junior for the defendant is seen to rise, without any ceremony, and to address the Court. In a stentorian voice, hardly according with the quiet tone common to the Court of Chancery, he declares:

> "Sir, notwithstanding the somewhat offhand and supercilious manner in which this case has been dealt with by my learned friend, Sir Roundell Palmer, and to some extent acquiesced in by my learned Leader, Mr. Kay, if, Sir, you will only listen to me, I pledge myself you will dismiss this case with costs."

The Vice Chancellor, Sir Roundell Palmer, and in fact the entire court room stare with astonishment at the audacity of the unknown speaker, who, oblivious to them all, launches forth upon a withering attack. Insisting that the United States could not approbate and reprobate—that it could not take the benefits of the agency without assuming the liabilities—he spends three hours building his powerful arguments.

In the end Vice Chancellor James does dismiss the suit with costs. Later his decision is affirmed on appeal.

The Junior was Judah P. Benjamin, and he had won his first case!

Although hard pressed for money, the new barrister strove to maintain his dignity at a high level. Few cases came to him at first, but he gave no one the opportunity to hold his services in low esteem. On one occasion a solicitor's messenger brought papers to him for an opinion, with a fee of five pounds marked on them. Mr. Benjamin left the file on his desk without touching it. A few days later the messenger called for the papers. Finding no opinion among them he returned and asked if there had been some mistake. Benjamin replied that there was no mistake; that the five pounds was for taking the papers in—not reading them. Shortly thereafter the Solicitor appeared with an additional fee of twenty-five pounds, and the opinion was forthcoming without delay. Sometime later the solicitor told Mr. Benjamin that the client involved had specifically requested the new barrister's opinion; Benjamin replied with a smile that if he had known such to be the case, his fee would have been twice as much.

Finding himself little occupied with trial work, he turned to writing. There was great need for a concise treatise on sale under the English Law, and he labored diligently to supply that need. In 1868, "Benjamin, On Sales" was published; it was recognized immediately as the classic upon this subject. There was tremendous demand for it, not only in England, but in America as well. Lawyers everywhere acknowledged that here indeed was a master's discussion of principles, rather than a mere crude collection of decisions. A second edition appeared in 1873; and a third, ten years later.

Shortly after the book was published, Baron Martin, when taking his seat one morning upon the Bench, asked to have Mr. Benjamin's work handed to him.

"Never heard of it, my Lord," said the Chief Clerk.

"Never heard of it!" stormed Sir Samuel Martin. "Mind that I never take my seat here again without that book by my side."

His book attracted wide attention, and his practice commenced to grow rapidly. He was already a "Palatine Silk" for the county of Lancaster, when he appealed for the rank of Queen's Counsel. So well had he impressed the House of Lords in arguing the case of "Potter vs. Rankin" that the powerful Lord Hatherly supported his petition. The fall of 1872 found Judah P. Benjamin a Queen's Counsel, attending the Court Levee of her Royal Majesty.

What a thrilling moment for one who only a few years earlier had been a penniless exile in a foreign land. His round, dark face was framed in a full-bottomed wig, the wings of which fell down on his shoulders. His long silk gown swung open as he walked, revealing the customary knee breeches and black silk stockings. Silver buckles shone from the tops of his patent leather pumps. The slight smile, which seemed never to have left him, broadened somewhat as he greeted his friendly colleagues of the Bar. What a wave of mingled emotions passed over him as he bowed low before the Great Queen and expressed his gratitude for her gracious kindness. Once more the dark clouds of adversity had melted into oblivion; once more the sun shone brightly upon Judah P. Benjamin.

He began to make more frequent trips to Paris and to lavish the benefits of his growing fortune on Natalie and Ninette. The latter was married on September 7th, 1874, to Captain Henri de Bousignac, a distinguished artillery officer, attached to the French general staff. Her father saw fit to present as a dowry all of the savings he had up until then accumulated at the British Bar. The picture of a man sixty-three years of age making such a sacrifice is nearly unbelievable. He describes the situation in a letter to his folks back in New Orleans with the simple statement: "By giving up all my savings, I have been able to settle on Ninette $3,000 a year, so that her future is now secure against want; and I must now begin to lay up a provision for the old age of my wife and myself."

His life in London was the usual one of a bachelor in chambers. He would dine at his club, the Junior Athenaeum; and later stroll with a cigar in his mouth into the billiard-room or the cardroom. Sometimes he would indulge in a game of whist, which he played exceptionally well, but as a rule he preferred to watch "the boys." He disliked working after dinner and, when hard pressed, preferred to postpone his meal until nine o'clock in order to complete his tasks first.

There were many such postponed meals in the year 1875. Business began to come to him fast and furious. He was now the vogue, being in great demand by solicitors and constantly specified by the actual clients. He was so much in demand that he could name his own price. When questioned as to how he managed to bring in such a large income, he jokingly replied: "First I charge a retainer; then I charge a reminder; next I charge a refresher; and then I charge a finisher."

After a time he proceeded to limit his practice by refusing to go into any other court than the House of Lords or the Privy Council, except for a fee of 100 guineas. His fee for a consultation at a client's home was 300 guineas. In the Privy Council he distinguished himself time and again by his masterful handling of Colonial appeals. Thoroughly versed in systems of the law other than the English, he held all those who opposed him at a great disadvantage. His evident superiority in this field was quickly recognized and brought him many briefs from various parts of the Empire. Of the fifteen Scotch appeals made during one year, Benjamin appeared in eight.

During the first year of his practice, his income had amounted to less than five hundred pounds. For each of the years from 1877 to 1882 his fees were in excess of fifteen thousand pounds. His total earnings in sixteen years at the British Bar came to nearly three-quarters of a million dollars.

The dignity with which he always conducted himself after his appointment as Queen's Counsel brought him universal respect. And when he failed to receive the courtesies which he felt were due him, he was quick to make plain his attitude.

On one occasion, when he was arguing in the House of Lords on the case of "London Bank vs. Ratcliffe," Lord Chancellor Selborne saw fit to interrupt him with a rude objection. Mr. Benjamin insisted on proceeding with his speech, as he had planned it. Whereupon Selborne remarked in an undertone "Nonsense!" Mr. Benjamin quietly tied up his papers, bowed gravely to the members on the Bench, and said "That is my case, my Lords"; he then turned and left the House. Upon the convening of court next day Lord Selborne noticed the absence of Mr. Benjamin and stated in open court that he certainly was not justified in applying the term, "Nonsense," to anything that fell from Mr. Benjamin. He requested the Junior in the case to convey his regrets that he should have used such an expression. Mr. Benjamin promptly wrote a friendly and cordial note of acknowledgment.

Probably the case which brought him the greatest publicity was his defense of the captain of the German ship, *Franconia*. He had to argue this matter before fourteen judges, presided over by the Lord Chief Justice of England. His handling of the fine points of international law that were involved called forth the acclaim of all the British newspapers. It is interesting to note that this particular case was a criminal one, whereas, for the most part, just as in the old Louisiana days, he confined himself to civil causes.

The varied nature of his past career and experiences brought Benjamin many of his leading cases. His knowledge of statesmanship and diplomacy, his familiarity with the different systems of law, his fluency in French and Spanish, all united to make him unique, even at one of the most distinguished bars in legal history.

The *American Law Record* stated in 1880: "He has

become the recognized leader of an institution, of all others the most exclusive and difficult in which to attain prominence and success. The briefs declined by him would double his income. We doubt if this has ever been equalled by any other aspirant for distinction at the English or American Bar."

CHAPTER IX
THE PEACEFUL END

During the years of Benjamin's greatness at the British Bar, Disraeli was Prime Minister. And it was inevitable that comparisons should be drawn between the two. Aside from the similarities in ancestry and successful achievements, the two had little in common. The English Premier gloried in a manner that included both the bombastic and the exotic; his explosive oratory and purple waistcoats characterized his startling visits to the House of Lords. A thoroughly different picture is conjured up when one recalls the modestly attired, soft spoken, and dignified little lawyer from the States. The colorful life of the one reflected itself in his appearance; the equally dramatic career of the other was denied by his retiring, quiet manner. In Benjamin's habits of life there was a good deal of the Southern temperament. He used to say of himself that he "loved to bask in the sun like a lizard." In spite of such protestations he was considered the hardest-working member of the London Bar.

He studiously avoided politics throughout his years in England. At one time he wrote home: "We are in the midst of the turmoil of a general election here, and it amuses me to look on, as I do not take the slightest part in politics and shall never again be induced to emerge from the quietude of private life. Half my brethren of the bar are candidates, and great efforts have been made to induce me to become a candidate. I laugh them off, and both sides claim me, because I belong to neither."

What political preference he did have inclined more to Gladstone than to Disraeli. He was an intense admirer of both.

During the year 1879 he spent much of his time in Paris; he was busy building a magnificent home there for Natalie. The mansion, located at 41 Avenue d'Jena, still stands, a silent witness to his generous indulgence. To the very end he continued to lavish upon his wife the luxuries which meant so much to her. She was grateful, of course, and always thought her "J. P." the very dearest of men. However, her deepest affections were all reserved for Ninette who was so like her mother in every respect. The warm nature and great depth of Benjamin's personality never received adequate response from his family. It was the one tragedy that he was unable to overcome.

He himself took great pride in the new home, the first he could really call his own since the happy days on "Belle Chasse Plantation." He was commencing to feel the weight of his years and began to long for a period of quiet retirement. This was soon made absolutely necessary for him by an unfortunate accident which occurred in May, 1880. In a foolish attempt to jump off a rapidly moving Parisian tram-car, he was thrown violently to the ground. His right arm was torn from the socket, the shoulder blade broken, and the left side of the forehead fractured. Were it not for his hat, which acted as a buffer, he probably would have been killed outright.

His recovery was surprisingly rapid, however, and the following winter saw him back at his desk in

London. He continued to practise thruout the Spring, but spent the Summer at Biarritz with his family. The doctors then began to advise his retiring completely, as they had noted a diabetic affliction in addition to some of the harmful effects which still remained from the Paris accident. He continued to practise for a time, but finally gave in. Directing his clerk to announce his retirement, he returned all briefs to his clients and repaid all fees in matters which he was unable to finish.

He was greatly surprised and deeply moved at the announcement from every London newspaper, with the *Times* at the head, that his retirement was a matter of national concern and regret. He wrote: "For the last few days I have hardly kept my eyes free from tears on reading the testimonials to the rectitude and honor of my professional conduct, such as no member of the English Bar has ever received."

The *Daily News* asserted: "The career of such a man is, say we, almost unexampled. Mr. Benjamin no doubt had friends in England who may have smoothed the way of some technical difficulties and hastened some honorary distinctions, but the reputation he has attained is not of the kind that friends can hasten or enemies can mar."

The London *Times* regretted that fear of offending the United States prevented the elevation to the Bench of the Ex-Confederate leader. "None could have been selected worthier than Mr. Benjamin of a distinction which usually crowns a practice like his."

The conservative *Law Times* was loud in its praise: "With the exception of Lord Justice Mellish, we think it may be said that no lawyer of the present generation can be put in the same category with Mr. Benjamin. That no man at the Bar can occupy the space occupied by him is absolutely certain."

But these were only the forerunners of the still greater tribute that was to be paid him. He was completely overcome with emotion when on February 28, 1883, he received the following letter from the Attorney-General of England:

"My dear Benjamin:

"I have before me a document signed by nearly every leading member of the English Bar, the contents of which I am requested to convey to you. These old friends of yours are anxious that you should afford them collectively, an opportunity of showing their friendship to you; and they trust you will be their guest on some occasion convenient to yourself. I hope you will understand our reasons for desiring thus to meet you. We do not forget how you came some seventeen years ago a stranger amongst us. We offered you then no insincere welcome, and in return, you have always, during those years of your sojourn with us, supported the honor and position of our profession, and have added much to the public estimation in which we are held. And so now when you leave us, your old associates are anxious to show and to tell you how much they value the friendship they know that even now they have not lost.

"I am, my dear Benjamin, yours most truly,

"HENRY JAMES."

Benjamin accepted the gracious invitation, overwhelmed at the unprecedented honor. The great banquet took place on Saturday evening, June 30th. Every luminary of the British legal profession was to be seen in the more than two hundred guests who crowded the hall of the Inner Temple. The Attorney-General, Sir Henry James, presided; on his left sat the Lord Chancellor, Lord Selborne; on his right was the guest of honor. Nearby were the Lord Chief Justice and the Master of the Rolls, both warm friends of Mr. Benjamin. It was indeed a brilliant gathering.

After the usual toast to the Queen, Sir Henry James rose once more to propose the health of Judah P. Benjamin:

"Tonight the Bench and Bar unite to bid farewell and to wish Godspeed to an old and valued comrade. Remarkable and unprecedented as this gathering is, still the causes which have occasioned it are easy to tell.

"You know how Mr. Benjamin came among us, and how we received him. 'Ejectum littore egentem accepimus'; but no regret, no self-reproach has ever come to us for having given him place within our kingdom. He knocked at our doors, and they were widely opened to him. We found place for him in our foremost rank; we grudged him not the leadership he so easily gained— we were proud of his success, for we knew the strength of the stranger among us, and the bar is ever generous, even in its rivalry, toward success that is based on merit.

"And the merit must have been there, for who is the man save this one of whom it can be said that he held conspicuous leadership at the bar of two countries? To him this change of citizenship and transition in his profession seemed easy enough. From the first days of his coming he was one of us. We had been taught by the same teachers, Cole and Blackstone. But he was one of us not only in this common knowledge. The honor of the English Bar was as much cherished and represented by him as by any man who has ever adorned it. We all feel that if our profession has afforded him hospitality, he has repaid it, amply repaid it, not only by the reputation which his learning has brought to us, but by that which is more important, the honor his conduct has gained for us.

"But he became one of us in fuller spirit yet; not only the lawyer but the man was of us. Rivalry with him seemed to create rather than to disturb friendship, and it was within the walls of our courts that Mr. Benjamin first found those friends who sit around him tonight. And how strange and quick must have been his power to make them!

"Mr. Benjamin sees here no small gathering of men who have come in friendship to his side. To other men it may be given also to have many friendships, but they take a lifetime to form. They commence in childhood and strengthen and increase as life goes on. The years are few since Mr. Benjamin was a stranger to us all, and in those few years he has accomplished more than most men can ever hope in a lifetime to achieve."

THE PEACEFUL END

The honored guest was deeply moved as he prepared to reply, and there were tears in his eyes. He spoke briefly and simply, sincerity ringing in every word: "The feelings of joy and gratification at this testimonial are counter-balanced—more than counter-balanced—by the reflection, unutterably sad, that to the large majority of those present my farewell words tonight are a final earthly farewell—that to the large majority of you I shall never again be cheered by the smiling welcome, by the hearty hand-grasp, with which I have been greeted during many years, and which had become to me almost the very breath of my life. It was on the 16th of December, 1832, that I was first called to the Bar; and on the 7th of December last I had accomplished fifty years of professional life."

The speaker dwelt for a moment on his illness and the causes of his retirement. Then, in saddened tones, continued:

"From the Bar of England I never, so far as I am aware, received anything but warm and kindly welcome. I never had occasion to feel that any one regarded me as an intruder. I never felt a touch of professional jealousy. I never received any unkindness. On the contrary, from all quarters I received a warm and cordial welcome to which, as a stranger, I had no title except that I was a political exile, seeking by honorable labor, to retrieve shattered fortunes, wrecked in the ruin of a Lost Cause.... I must conclude by thanking you all from the bottom of my heart for the kind reception you have given me ever since I first came among you down to this magnificent testimonial, the recollection of which will never fade from my memory, and on which I shall always love to dwell. I thank you all."

. . . . . .

The career in England was at an end. His London offices were closed; his affairs had been set in order. He had followed his lifelong custom of destroying nearly all his papers by the time he departed for Paris.

Through the Summer of 1883 his health improved slightly, but whatever progress had been made was quickly lost during the severe winter which followed. "If we can only get rid of this glacial temperature and dry east wind, I shall get some strength. What I require is warmth—will it never come?"

He continued to fail, tho maintaining a cheerful attitude to the very end. The warm sun was just beginning to return, when on May 6th the fine old gentleman passed away.

They buried him without ostentation in Père la Chaise Cemetery, following a simple service at the Church of St. Pierre de Chaillot. Natalie was anxious that he receive the last rites of her faith; and tho Benjamin never forsook his ancestral religion, the manner in which his funeral was conducted should make little difference. He had a fine, quiet pride in his race and its religious convictions that transcended the outward ceremonials of his own or any other faith. "The brotherhood of man" was the formula he adhered to; and as to whether pastor, priest, or rabbi consecrated his funeral, it could really have made little difference to him.

He left his family well provided for, even devising large legacies for his relatives back in New Orleans. It was the third great fortune he had carved out during his lifetime. The first had been swept away by the failure of the "Belle Chasse" venture and the simultaneous other mishaps. The second had gone down with the fallen star of the Confederacy. The third was more than ample to take care of those he left behind.

The modest notice that appeared in the British *Law Times* of May 17, 1884, was in harmony with the simple tastes of the man whom it eulogized. It was placed in an obscure corner; it was headed in quiet fashion "The Late Mr. Benjamin, Q. C."; but its text was a glowing tribute:

"One of the most remarkable of modern careers came to an end on Tuesday with the death of Mr. Judah Philip Benjamin. His parents were English Jews; he was born in the West Indies, on the island of St. Thomas; was an attorney of Louisiana, a Senator of the United States, and the Secretary of State for the Southern Confederation. He became an English journalist, barrister, Queen's Counsel, and Bencher at Lincoln's Inn; at length he took up his residence in Paris where he died.

"His life was as varied as an Eastern tale and he carved out for himself not one but three several histories of great and well-earned distinction. The secret of this remarkable success is told in a few pregnant words by a leader of men who gave practical effect to the highest possible estimate of Mr. Benjamin's ability.

" 'Mr. Benjamin,' wrote Jefferson Davis, 'had impressed me with the lucidity of his intellect, his systematic habits, and his capacity for labor.'

"But to these qualities must be added indomitable faith in the future and a courage which no reverses could dampen. The stars in their courses fought against Judah Benjamin, but he struggled on until the sun, in which he loved, he said, 'to bask like a lizard,' came out and gave him new prosperity.

"Mr. Francis Galton has shown that legal ability is hereditary, as is indicated by the names of the Montagues, the Norths, the Coleridges, the Pollocks, and the Denmans; no less inherited is that elastic resistance to evil fortune which preserved Mr. Benjamin's ancestors through a succession of exiles and plunderings, and reappeared in the great Minister of the Confederate Cause."

ACKNOWLEDGEMENT

THE author wishes to record his deep indebtedness to the following secondary sources: "Judah P. Benjamin," by Pierce Butler; "Judah P. Benjamin, Distinguished at the Bars of Two Nations," an article by James Winston; "Judah P. Benjamin, Statesman and Jurist," a monograph by Max Kohler; "Memorials of Eminent Yale Men," by Anson Phelps Stokes.

The primary sources used include manuscripts in the possession of the Yale University Library; the Cabildo at New Orleans; the Confederate Museum and the Virginia State Library, both in Richmond. The newspaper files of the Yale Library and of the British Museum Reading Room in London were particularly valuable. In Paris, the Bibliothéque Nationale and the interment records of Père la Chaise Cemetery were consulted.

ACKNOWLEDGEMENT

The historical background was constructed with the aid of various of the "Chronicles of America Series," edited by Allen Johnson. The following works of varied descriptions were likewise employed: "Yale College," by William L. Kingsley; "New Orleans, as I Found It," by H. Didimus; "Louisiana, Robinson Law Reports, Vol. X"; "De Bow's Review, Vols. II and V"; "The United States and Mexico," by J. Fred Rippy; "The Whig Party in the South," by Arthur Charles Cole; "Modern Eloquence, Vol. XI"; "Congressional Globe"; "Rise and Fall of the Confederate Government," by Jefferson Davis; "A Rebel War Clerk's Diary," by J. B. Jones; "Messages and Papers of the Confederacy," by Richardson; and others.

Furthermore there should be added the personal thanks of the author to many kind friends. These include Professor Ralph Henry Gabriel of the Yale History Department; Mr. Andrew Keogh and Mrs. James Ingersoll of the Yale University Library; Miss Josephine Cerf of the Cabildo, at New Orleans; Miss India Thomas of the Confederate Museum, in Richmond;

Mr. Herbert Ezekiel, officer in the Sons of the Confederacy, at Richmond. And finally my wife and mother, who vied with each other in patiently following every line.

INDEX

INDEX

Abbeville, 160
Abolitionists, 39, 70
Adams, Charles Francis, 143, 144
Adams Street, 121
Alabama Claims, 144
Albemarle Sound, 133
Almonte, 148
Amsterdam, 26, 27
Arista, President of Mexico, 87
Avenue de Jéna, No. 41, 184

Barlow, S. M., 38
Baton Rouge, 77
Bayard, Senator, 102
Belle Chasse Plantation, 48, 58-62, 185
Bemini Isles, 163
Benjamin, Bradford, and Finney, firm of, 103
Benjamin, Harriet, 30
Benjamin, Joseph, 30
Benjamin, Judah Philip: Speech of Dec. 1861, 19; ancestry, 25-28; early training, 29; Yale activities, 31-37; courtship and marriage, 44; admission to bar, 46; early legal triumphs, 49; period of despondency, 56; achievements as a sugar planter, 59-60; entrance to public life, 63; public orations, 71-73; election to U. S. Senate, 76; Louisiana-Tehuantepec Co., 81-94; Southern leader in Senate, 94-103; varied legal activities, 103-106; final speeches in Senate, 110-116; Attorney-General of Confederacy, 118-124; Secretary of War, 124-136; Secretary of State, 136-140; diplomacy, 141-158; flight from Richmond, 159; escape to England, 161-166; admission to British Bar, 170; "Benjamin on Sales," 176; Legal Triumphs in England, 177-181; comparison with Disraeli, 182; honored by British Bar, 186-192; serious accident, 185; last illness, 192; death, 193; interment, 193
Benjamin, Julia, 30
Benjamin, Natalie St. Martin, 44-48, 74, 166, 178, 184, 193
Benjamin, Ninette, 48, 166, 178, 185
Benjamin, Penina, 30
Benjamin, Philip, 27-30, 40
Benjamin, Rebecca de Mendes, 28, 30, 56, 60
Benjamin, Solomon, 30
"Benjamin, On Sales," 176
Biarritz, 186
Birney, 69
Black, Secretary, 109
Blackstone, 190
Blaine, James G., 95
Boardman, John D., 37
Bourbon St., 47

British Bar, 166-171, 177-184, 186-191
Brothers in Unity Debating Society, 31-33
Brougham, Lord, 168
Buchanan, President, 108, 109

Cairnes, Sir Hugh, 168
Calhoun, John C., 116
California Land Commissioners, Case of, 103
Calliope Debating Society, 31, 32
Cambridge, 169
Campbell, Lord, 167
Capston, Lieut. J. L., 150-154
Cass, General, 96
Cavour, 116
Charleston, 29, 30, 40
Charlotte, 160
Chase, Senator, 95
Chihuahua, 149
Clay, Henry, 31, 63, 64, 69, 98
Code Napoléon, 172
Cole, 190
Coleridges, the, 195
Colombian Republic, 83
Colonial Appeals, 179
Conrad, Congressman, 121
Creole Case, 51-56
Creole defined, 46
Crittenden, J. J., 106
Cromwell, Oliver, 27
Cuba, 164
Cuban filibusters, 104
Curry, J. L. M., 99

Danville, 159
Davenport home, 121
Davis, Jefferson, 102, 103, 107, 111, 117, 122-124, 136-139, 156, 159-161, 165
Davis, Mrs. Jefferson, 139, 155
Day, President Jeremiah of Yale, 34, 36, 39
deBousignac, Captain Henri, 178

DeBow's Review, 58, 59
Democratic Party, 98
Denmans, the, 195
Dirmmock, Col. Charles, 129-132
Disraeli, Benjamin, 24, 167, 183, 184
d'Israeli, Benjamin the elder, 27
Donelson, Fort, 132
Douglas, Senator, 95
Dred Scott Decision, 99

Ecuador, 104
Emancipation Proclamation, 143
England, 27, 54, 120, 141-146, 165, 167-172, 180, 186-192
Erlanger, 147
Everett, Senator, 95
Exchange Hotel, 119

Fayetteville Academy, 29
Ferguson, Sir James, 167
Florida, 162
Foote, Gov., 147
Forsyth, U. S. Minister to Mexico, 91, 93
France, 48, 141, 146-149, 166, 178
Franconia Case, 181
Freeman's Journal, 152
French Code, 50
Fugitive Slave Law, 64
Fushee Street, 121

Gag Law, 69
Galapagos Islands, 104
Galton, Francis, 195
Garay, Don José, 83-85
Garibaldi, 116
Gettysburg, 144, 154
Gladstone, 143, 184
Gorgas, Lieut. Col., 131
Grant, Gen. Ulysses S., 132, 155
Greensboro, 160
Grymes, John K., 50

Haiti, 46
Hargous, P. A., 85

INDEX

Hatherly, Lord, 177
Hatteras, 133
Havana, 164
Henderson, General, 104
Henry, Patrick, 115
Hoge, Rev. Dr., 159
Holt, Secretary, 109
Horace, 139
Huger, General Benjamin, 133
Hunt, Randell, 76
Huntington Brothers, 62

Ireland, 150
Iron clad rams, 144

Jackson, General Stonewall, 129
Jacksonian Democracy, 64
James, Sir Henry, 188-190
James, Vice Chancellor, 173-175
Johnson, Reverdy, 105, 106
Johnston, General Albert S., 132
Johnston, General Joseph E., 129, 160
Johnston, J. M., 159
Juarez, 93, 149
Junior Athenaeum Club, 178
Justinian, 172

Kansas-Nebraska Bill, 97
Kay, Mr., 173
Kenner, Duncan, 76, 121, 157, 158
Keyes, General E. D., 111
Know Nothing Party, 152

Lamb Buildings, No. 4, 171
La Sère, Emile, 91, 92
Lee, General Robert E., 135, 156
Letcher, Governor John, 126, 130
Letcher, U. S. Minister to Mexico, 87
Levy, Mrs. Abraham (Rebecca Benjamin), 30, 60
Lewis, Sir George, 24
Liberty Party, 69
Lincoln, President Abraham, 93, 108, 110, 120, 155-157

Lincoln's Inn, 168-170
Linonia Debating Society, 31
Liverpool, 173
London, 24, 27, 167-172, 186-192
London Bank vs. Ratcliffe, case of, 180
Lopez, Moses, 29, 30
Louisiana, 46, 49, 51, 57, 58, 64, 67, 80, 121

Main Street, 121
Mainning and MacIntosh, firm of, 85
Mallory, S. R., 140
Manassas, first battle of, 123
Marshall, Col. Charles, 135
Martin, Sir Samuel, 176
Mason, J. M., 50, 140, 144, 145, 149, 157, 173
Maximilian, 149
Mazureau, 50
Mazzini, 116
McCargo vs. The New Orleans Insurance Co., case of, 52
McClane, U. S. Minister to Mexico, 93
McCulloch, Professor R. S., 59
McDonogh's Will, case of, 105
McIver, Rev. Colin, 29
Mellish, Lord Justice, 187
Memminger, C. G., 140
Mercier, 146
Mexico, 82-94, 148
Michaelmas Term, 173
Micou and Benjamin, firm of, 103
Mill, John Stuart, 142
Missouri Compromise, 31
Mix, Mr., 32
Montagues, the, 195
Montesquieu, 71
Montgomery, 119-121
Murphy, Dennis, 95

Napoleon III, 146, 148, 149
Nassau, 53, 163
Native American Party, 64

New Haven, 40
New Orleans, 40-44, 46, 62, 66, 71, 77
Norfolk, 53
Norths, the, 195

O'Connor, Charles S., 38, 106
Ostend Manifesto, 50
Overend, Gurney and Co., 168
Oxford, 169

Packwood, 59
Palmer, Sir Roundell, 168, 174
Palmerston, 142-145, 158
Pamlico, 133
Papal Intervention, 154
Paris, 42, 166, 178, 184, 185, 193
Peachey, A. C., 106
Père la Chaise Cemetery, 193
Pierce, President Franklin, 106
Pollock, Charles, 170
Pollocks, the, 195
Polymnia Street, 62
Pontalba, Mme. de, 166
Potter vs. Rankin, case of, 177
Preston, William, 148
Privy Council, 172, 179

Quintero, 148
Quitman, 104
Quito, 104

Randolph, G. W., 140
Reagan, J. H., 140
Rembrandt, 26
Republican Party, 98
Richmond, 121, 124-135, 140, 146, 150, 155, 159
Richmond Light Infantry Blues, 122
Rillieux, 58
Roanoke Island, 132-137
Roebuck, 143
Russell, 143

St. Charles Island, 104
St. Martin, Auguste, 45, 60

St. Martin, Jules, 121
St. Paul's Church, 159
St. Pierre de Chaillot, 193
St. Thomas, 28, 165
Santa Anna, President of Mexico, 83
Santo Domingo, 42, 46
Scott, General Winfield, 111
Selborne, Lord Chancellor, 180, 188
Sephardic Communities, 26
Seward, Senator and Secretary of State, 95, 97, 99, 100, 149
Sherbrooke, Lord, 24
Sherman, General William, 155
Slidell, John, 50, 147, 157, 166
Slidell, Thomas, 49, 50, 52
Smith, General Kirby, 164
Sonora, 149
Soulé, Pierre, 50, 80
South Carolina, Secession of, 108-110
Spain, 25
Spinoza, 26
Stanton, Secretary, 109
Stringer, Greenbury R., 44
Stuart, Capt., 164
Sugar refining, 57-60
Sumner, Senator, 95
Sumter, Fort, 39, 109, 119, 120

Taney, Chief Justice, 100
Tehuantepec Railroad, 81-94
Tennyson, 139, 160, 161
The Temple, 171
Toussaint L'Ouverture, 46
Trent Affair, 143
Trist, 85
"Twenty Years in Congress," 95

United States vs. McRae, case of, 173-175

Vanderbilt, Commodore, 83
Vest, Senator, 95
Vicksburg, 144, 154
Victoria, Queen, 177
Villamil, General, 104

INDEX

Wade, Senator, 95, 101
Walker, Leroy P., 119, 124
Washington, George, 115
Washington, Georgia, 160
Watts, T. H., 140
Webster, Daniel, 63, 87, 98, 123

Whig Party, 63, 64, 66-68, 76, 98
Whiting, General William H., 128
Wilmington, 29
Wise, General Henry A., 133-136

Yale College, 30-38

Printed in the USA
CPSIA information can be obtained
at www.ICGtesting.com
LVHW091321281023
762073LV00025B/20